OPEN
NET

OPEN NET

GEORGE PLIMPTON

THE LYONS PRESS
Guilford, Connecticut
An imprint of The Globe Pequot Press

Copyright © 2003 by George Plimpton

All rights reserved. No part of this book may be reproduced or transmitted in any form by any means, electronic or mechanical, including photocopying and recording, or by any information storage and retrieval system, except as may be expressly permitted in writing from the publisher. Requests for permission should be addressed to The Lyons Press, Attn: Rights and Permissions Department, P.O. Box 480, Guilford, CT 06437.

The Lyons Press is an imprint of The Globe Pequot Press

10 9 8 7 6 5 4 3 2 1

Printed in the United States of America

ISBN 1-59228-120-6

Library of Congress Cataloging-in-Publication Data is available on file.

FOR OAKES, PAT, ROBIN,
AND SAINT LYDWINA OF SCHIEDEN

The pratfall on ice, it has been said, is the great leveling experience of saints and sinners. Indeed, the patron saint of skaters, Saint Lydwina of Schieden, is shown wearing skates in an early fifteenth-century Dutch woodcut, collapsed on the ice, and being helped to her feet by two friends. On this occasion, according to theological teachings, she broke a rib, which was among the first of a horrifying succession of physical ailments she suffered for almost forty years, bearing them with such legendary fortitude that she was eventually canonized. That she is the patron saint of the skater (and very likely the accident-prone as well) is hardly surprising considering the nature of the sport. Neither an easy name to remember nor to shout ("Oh, Saint Lydwina of Schieden!") during the course of a tumble on ice, she is acknowledged here since her presence seems to be evident in much of what follows.

G. A. P.

ACKNOWLEDGMENTS

This book covers an extended period of time—from the late summer of 1977, when I joined the Bruins' training camp, to the spring of 1985, when I went to Edmonton to look in briefly on the Oilers. The game of hockey has seen substantial changes, both tactically and in the outlook of players; my hope has been to record some of these, along with describing my own somewhat limited experiences in the sport. Hockey is wondrously rich with characters and stories, and the legend keepers capable of recounting them are many. I am especially grateful to Harry Sinden, the general manager of the Bruins, Don Cherry, the coach at the time, and in particular the Boston goaltenders, Gerry Cheevers and, of course, Jim Pettie, my roommate at the training camp. All of the Bruins' so-called Lunch-Pail Gang were at once solicitous and informative, especially Mike Milbury, Rick Smith, John Wensink, and ex-Bruins Phil Esposito and Bobby Orr. Two other organizations were extremely helpful—the Philadelphia Flyers, who allowed me the chance to experience a confrontation in the Spectrum, and the Oilers, who granted me the privilege of joining them for a short period in Edmonton. Two experts in the field, Stu Hackel and Craig Wolff, went over versions of the text and were helpful with their criticisms and advice.

And, of course, I am indebted to those at W. W. Norton most closely involved with the project—Ed Barber, Hilary Hinzmann, Andy Marasia, and Nina Bouis—as well as to Mark Mulvoy, the editor of *Sports Illustrated,* who initiated the series that has grown into this volume.

INTRODUCTION

When *Open Net* was first published, it received generally good reviews, especially in Boston, as might be expected. In Detroit, the *Free Press* described it as "one of the best hockey books ever written." The other Detroit paper, however, the *News*, did not agree. Its reviewer, Stanley Fischler, picked on one or two inaccuracies, and ended his critique by warning his readers off "this dreadful book." Mr. Fischler has sturdy credentials. He is the author of dozens of works on hockey, many of them "as told to" books with star players. He has been a color commentator on television for the New York Islanders. It was dismaying to be taken to task by such an authority. His fastidiousness simply could not allow him to appreciate the whole. Or the humor. Sympathetic sportswriters told me not to fret about it—it was a matter of Mr. Fischler not being at all comfortable with someone else tramping about in his fiefdom, especially someone with limited credentials.

Still, that dreadful word "dreadful" rankled and did so for quite a time. Then, a few years ago I found myself sitting up in the "blue seats" of Madison Square Garden at a game between the Rangers and the Islanders. These are the seats in the uppermost tiers of the Garden and are known for the raucous behavior of its occupants. I had done an article on the blue-seat fans for *Sports Illustrated*, quite sympathetic since it had seemed to me that their behavior, often manifested in obscene chants, was vaguely justified since it stemmed out of loyalty and the frustration that the Rangers hadn't won a Stanley Cup since

1940. They were true fans. They had appreciated the *Sports Illustrated* article, and thus I was welcomed up there. When the Bruins came to town I was even allowed to carry a small Bruins pennant up into that beer-drenched aerie and wave it on occasion, if not too often.

I would not have been able to do this if I had been an Islander fan. One night at the Garden during a Rangers-Islander game, a fan—very likely on a dare—ventured into the "blues" wearing an Islander jersey. He was set upon and divested not only of the jersey but just about everything else. The jersey was tossed contemptuously toward the Islander bench.

The reason for this animosity goes back to February, 1979, when an Islander player, Dennis Potvin, checked a Ranger star, Ulf Nilson, into the boards and in the process broke Ulf's ankle, an injury that Ranger fans to this day consider to have deprived them of a Stanley Cup. Though the check was clean and no penalty was meted out, Potvin was for years considered the devil incarnate and indeed, though he has long retired, continues to be. At every game in the Garden (and often elsewhere in the league) from somewhere in the arena a curious sequence of whistles begins to sound, gathering momentum, which ignites a bellow from the initiated: *Potvin Sucks!"* In other arenas the response to the introductory whistle is obviously rather muted—a few displaced Ranger fans rising to the call. In the Garden, however, the response is thunderous—at least from the blue seats. Actually, authorities tell me many fans have no idea what the cry refers to (it happened so long ago)—as if indulging in a kind of holy incantation in a mysterious foreign language.

In any case, that night during the Islander-Ranger game I asked my neighbor—a considerable force in the blue seats—if it were possible to substitute another name for Potvin. I told him how Stan Fischler had savaged *Open Net.* His eyes popped at the audacity. Word spread through the blue seats. The introductory whistle started up and to my delight the cry rang throughout the Garden: *"Fischler Sucks!"* It was done again. I have no idea whether its target heard the cry, but I hold to the rather sniggling hope that he did.

Now the slate is wiped clean. It means that if I am asked to review one of Stan Fischler's books, I can do so with an open mind!

—George Plimpton
August, 1993

1

THERE was one major sport I thought I would never find myself involved in as a participatory journalist. Ice hockey. I had what seemed a logical excuse: I am very poor on skates. I tend to skate on my ankle bones. Someone once pointed out that on skates I am the same height *off* as I am on the ice. It was odd, because much of my adolescence I spent in New England where in wintertime one puts on skates and gets out on the frozen ponds as a matter of course. But I was no good at it. I have heard people insist —and indeed every instructional manual on skating repeats it—that there is no such phenomenon as "weak ankles," that if the child skates on his ankle bones it is because the skates are too large, or have not been laced up properly. I have always been a refutation of that argument. As a youngster I shoved off from the banks of the pond very nearly on four points—however snug and well-laced the skates—so that my skating style was not unlike someone walking along half-in and half-out of a pair of galoshes. I improved as time went on, but not markedly: the only time I was truly erect on my skates, the blades immediately under my weight, was when I stopped the frantic shuffling that had gained me my speed and did some gliding—cruising along, wobbling slightly, but quite aloft, with just a faint wash of wind in my face which slowly died away as my momentum slowed. The skates would then flop over onto the ice—rather like the settling down of a spinning top. Again I would start the scuttling motion to work up some speed. There was always advice from people who watched this stop-and-go advance along the ice. "You need to wear another pair of socks," they would say.

So when the editors of *Sports Illustrated* called and said the Boston Bruins were willing to take me on for part of the training season up at their camp at Fitchburg, Massachusetts, I winced and said I wasn't sure my skating was up to it.

"How long do I have to get ready?"

"A couple of weeks."

"I'm very skeptical."

"You can play in the goal."

"The goal?"

Mark Mulvoy, who was the magazine's hockey writer at the time and is now its editor, remarked over the phone that I should remember the sentiment that had motivated Tretiak, the great Russian goaltender, namely "that there is no position in sport as noble as that of goaltending."

I replied that I had no wish to be ennobled, especially at the expense of my front teeth.

"We'll find you a mask. One more thing."

"What's that?" I asked.

"About a month after you report to Fitchburg, the Bruins have an exhibition game in the Spectrum against the Philadelphia Flyers. You'll be allowed in to play for a while."

"Allowed in?"

"The Bruins will put you in the goal for about five minutes," he said, ". . . to see what will happen."

I asked: "Isn't there someone on the Flyers named 'The Hammer'?"

"Schultz," Mulvoy said. "An enforcer. The King of the Goons. He is no longer with them, you'll be pleased to hear, but he has left rafts of disciples."

"Oh yes."

"You'd better do something about your skating," Mulvoy said as he hung up the phone.

Almost as soon as we had finished talking, I looked into the yellow pages of the telephone directory to check out an ice rink. I marked down the name of the Skyrink on Manhattan's West Side, near an entrance to the Lincoln Tunnel. Then I went down to Cosby's sports store next to Madison Square Garden. There I bought a pair of goalie's skates— which are low to the ice with thick cuplike guards over the toes and extra flanges attached to the skate blades to keep a puck from slipping through. I also purchased a protective face mask, trying it on and staring at myself in a mirror through the eye slits.

That same evening I dropped in on the Skyrink to try everything out. The Wurlitzer organ was playing "Waltzing Matilda." Extraordinarily capable people sailed by, the men with hands clasped comfortably behind their backs, chins thrust out, and dreamlike expressions on their faces, while at center ice the young women pirouetted in tight circles, most of them very young girls with their heads thrown back and their pony tails hanging down and swinging as they turned. I stepped out onto the ice in my goaltender's skates and to my surprise found myself creeping along the sideboards like the frightened rat, Chuchundra, in Rudyard Kipling's *Rikki-tikki-tavi,* who never dares to come into the middle of the room . . . taking crotchety steps as I tried to dredge out of my past even the simplest fundamentals. I had forgotten everything . . . how to stop . . . to skate backwards. I had always assumed that once one had learned to skate, it was inevitably there—however awkwardly one did it

. . . like bicycling, or remembering how to play "Chop-
sticks," or swimming, or folding a sheet of paper to build
a glider. But all that was left of my skating past, with its
crazy abandon, was that I still sagged over onto my ankle
bones. Some of the skaters whizzing by glanced curiously
down at my goalie's skates as I moved slowly over the ice.
Could any of them have imagined that they were looking
at someone who in a few weeks' time would be playing for
the Boston Bruins?

I went back to the Skyrink evening after evening—
grimly circling the ice until things began to improve. Sometimes I glided to a stop and hunched down in front of an
imaginary goal. I tried the quick lateral movements I knew
would be required of the goal tender. What could my skating companions at the rink have made of this—a solitary
figure hopping and shifting back and forth across a small
rectangular area of ice . . . ?

I haunted the strange neon glow of the place. I came to
know its hierarchy, which was established in circles, like the
rings of an immense archery target. On the outside were the
unwashed, the clumsies, the shriekers, the flailers, the board
clutchers, the small tots who took six quick walking steps
and then glided, teetering slightly, for three yards. It was
in this first circle that I had toiled during my early visits,
towering above the children, until slowly, as the sessions
went on, I gained confidence and worked my way gingerly
into the inner rings. Here the movement was quicker and
more professional. Skaters moved in rhythm to the music,
their skates biting into the ice on the turns. Among us
moved a speed skater with his long blades, and, on occasion, an older couple, wonderfully proficient, the man very
natty, with a small white moustache, and the woman with
a woolen skating dress of scotch plaid with a big decorative
safety pin, both with gloves and holding hands to do the

dance turns as the waltz poured out over us from the Wurlitzer.

In from us was the sacrosanct center oval in which the figure skaters performed—the girls in pert skirts that lifted when they twirled, their shanks extended by the height of their skates, so that their long-legged enchantment was exaggerated, like the romanticized heroines in a space-age comic strip. There was invariably a child prodigy or two— thin, stilt-like girls, beautifully kempt, and often so young as to be barely on the edge of being able to talk, each as spangled as toy poodles, and launched out onto the ice by young mothers who never took their eyes off their daughters and who sat waiting on the benches with the straw picnic baskets that contained their suppers.

Out in the center, the faces of the skaters were bland with concentration, either about what moves they were about to execute, or, more likely, in egocentric consideration of what an enviable spectacle they presented to the rest of us —we lesser moons to their planetary brilliance. One had only to see one of these estimable creatures stumble and have her bottom slide a swatch across the faint snow coating on the ice to know the true misery of the pratfall. This rarely seemed to happen, though those of us on the perimeter wistfully wished it happened more. The girls jumped up with slight frowns, very brief, and were immediately as composed and superior as members of a royal court, which of course they were, with only a slight tuft of ice shavings on their rumps to show that anything untoward had happened.

One evening, as I was seated on one of the long benches, skates off and working my toes back and forth, a man skated off the rink and sat down next to me. He asked if I would like to stay after the public had left the rink and play some midnight hockey. Oh yes, he went on, that was a regular

tradition. There was actually a team that played out of the
Skyrink—Gitler's Gorillas.

"The Gorillas."

The man nodded and said that he had noticed my skates.
"Goalie, eh?" He told me that their regular goalie had just
telephoned to say that his butcher's shop in Kew Gardens
had been damaged by fire the night before and he was still
taking inventory. He could not make it for that night's
scrimmage. Would I take his place? His question came just
as I was imagining the barbecue smell of cooked steak
drifting above Kew Gardens.

"Well, I don't know," I said. My mind raced. "I'm not
really a goalie. I'm *learning* to be a goalie." I could not
bring myself to tell him what team I was getting myself
ready to play for . . . it would have seemed such an imperti-
nence to drop the Boston Bruins' name on top of Gitler's
Gorillas.

He told me it was all very informal and friendly. Among
the people who came to the rink at midnight were a jazz
vibraphonist, two or three stockbrokers, a magazine writer,
a chef, an antique-furniture restorer, and, of course, the
goaltending butcher from Kew Gardens. One of the Gorillas, my friend told me, was a bell captain at the Plaza Hotel.
That grand place has since seemed slightly less imperious
and toney for knowing that one of its gold-button-fronted
entrance custodians is sailing around the Skyrink, banging
his stick on the ice for the puck, at one A.M.

He told me something about the organization. The foun-
der was a jazz entrepreneur named Ira Gitler who formed
the Gorillas (utilizing the Great Ape moniker for allitera-
tive nicety) in the spring of 1973. Actually, I was told, his
wife was better known in hockey circles—a sculptress spe-
cializing in life-size assemblages of sports figures—most of
them hockey stars wearing real pads and wielding North-

land or Koho hockey sticks. Her work turns up in corporate headquarters and banks. I was told a particularly dynamic assemblage recreated a Derek Sanderson and Orland Kurtenbach fight in the late 1960s.

"Is the assemblage realistic?" I asked. "Can you recognize Sanderson?"

"It's difficult," I was told. "Kurtenbach's hands are in Derek's face. But it is realistic. Kurtenbach suffered a skin condition and in the sculpture you can see that he's wearing a gray medicinal glove."

I stayed to watch them scrimmage. The Gorillas, or perhaps their opponents—the varied jerseys and sweat shirts gave no hint of a common identity—appeared about half an hour before midnight with big equipment bags. They sat down heavily on the long green rinkside benches. With their leg pads, the white plastic helmets, and the rest of the hockey accoutrements, they seemed a world removed from the long-legged girls still spinning their last pirouettes in the center of the ice—rather like the football players on the edge of the field, limbering up, settling their helmets into place, while the majorettes with the little pompoms on their sneakers are still kicking up their long legs and the silver batons are twirling in the sky.

"Have you had any . . . er . . . clumsies out there playing on the Gorillas?"

My companion looked up briefly into the rafters of the rink. "Well, we had this lawyer who came out one night, a real Rangers fan, entirely dressed up in Rangers regalia, even the Rangers colors, red and blue, on his helmet. After a couple of strides in a scrimmage he fell down and broke a collarbone. I'm not sure anyone even got his name. We supported him off. I helped. I remember the new crisp feeling of his hockey jersey."

I finally succumbed and told my friend from the Gorillas

why I was there—that I was preparing for a stint with the Boston Bruins. He did not seem especially surprised. In fact, he mentioned that to scrimmage with Gitler's Gorillas was just the way to round into shape to show the Bruins a thing or two when I got up to their training camp.

I agreed. But I also demurred. I told myself that if I should happen to get hurt playing with them and somebody asked, "What's happened to the right side of your face?" it was one thing to reply, "Slap shot . . . off the stick of Wayne Cashman of the Boston Bruins," and quite another to report that the deed had been done by the doorman of the Plaza Hotel during a scrimmage involving Gitler's Gorillas.

"I'm not quite ready yet for the Gorillas," I told my friend. "For the time being, I'll just watch."

W H I L E my evenings were taken up with skating sessions at the Skyrink, I prepared for Fitchburg in more sedentary ways. I did considerable reading—instruction manuals (especially on goaltending) and various biographies of hockey personalities. I kept notes. Also I thought a lot about the protective face mask I had bought at Cosby's. My notion was to get it decorated in such a way that would perhaps give the opposition a slight start, as well as providing me with a small psychological boost.

The face mask has been around since November 2, 1959 (I wondered if I ever would have had the nerve to accept playing in the goal if such things were not available), when the Montreal Canadiens' Jacques Plante introduced his in a game against the New York Rangers in New York's Madison Square Garden. Plante had a wonderful excuse: "I already had four broken noses, a broken jaw, two broken cheekbones, and almost 200 stitches in my head. I didn't care how the mask looked. I was afraid I would look just like the mask, the way things were going."

Incredibly, his colleagues looked upon Plante with scorn for wearing such a thing—derisive comments were made that he had gone soft. The fans did not think much better of him. One of them once asked Plante: "Doesn't the fact that you're wearing a mask *prove* that you're afraid?" In reply, Plante produced a most appropriate analogy: "If you jumped out of a plane without a parachute, would that *prove* you're brave?"

But however logical Plante was, no one seemed convinced. Chief among his critics was his own coach, Toe Blake, who tried incessantly to get Plante to discard his mask, only giving in when Plante said just as vehemently that he wouldn't skate out onto the ice without it.

Now, every goaltender wears one. The last goaltender to play without a mask was Andy Brown of the Detroit Red Wings . . . which so worried one of his female fans that before every game she sent him "lucky cookies" and sprigs of heather.

Since Plante introduced his mask in 1959, a number of goalies have taken the trouble to decorate them, usually with the team colors. The most famous mask was undoubtedly that of Gerry Cheevers, the first-string goalie on the Bruins team I was about to join, which was decorated with stitch marks painted on to depict the real ones Cheevers might have required if he had been playing with his face unprotected. In the locker room, very often still shaken by the concussion of the puck striking the mask, he would say, "Well, that was worth about eight," and the trainer, a man named Frosty Foristal, would draw a replica of that many stitches on the mask with a felt pen.

There were others. Gilles Gratton—a goaltender who

played for the New York Rangers—had an impressive
lion's head painted on his mask in deep vermilion. It turned
out that the lion's head was not so much to instill dismay in
the opponents as to reflect Gratton's interest in astrology:
he was born under the sign of Leo. Gratton had a turn of
mind interested in such things: he believed in reincarna-
tion; he told his Rangers teammates that during his life in
Biblical times he had stoned some people to death.

Was that so? his teammates had asked.

Yes, and that was why in this life he had ended up playing
goal.

When his teammates looked confused and asked about
the connection, Gratton replied that in his system of things
the good and bad were paid back in later lives, and because
he had made the mistake of once stoning people he was now
paying for it by having to stand in the goal mouth and
being, in a sense, stoned, inflicted by what he referred to
as a "plague of pucks."

He was quite a character. He believed he had been a
sixteenth-century soldier, stabbed to death. He had been
an archduke. In his present incarnation he had once
"streaked" the Maple Leaf Gardens—soaring out of the
wooden gate in the sideboards naked and doing a turn
around the ice at full speed before the startled crowd before
he disappeared. At least that is what I had heard. Perhaps
he had done it on a dare, or a bet. He would be someone
to check out once I joined the Bruins.

There were one or two other imaginatively decorated
masks I had heard about. One was Gary Simmons's of the
Los Angeles Kings. He had a green cobra painted on his
which I had assumed was to startle people, or at least to
illustrate his connection with the Kings—the King Cobra.
But not at all. Apparently, Simmons had a thing about
cobras. He had one tattooed on his right calf; he liked to

be called "Cobra." "Hey, Cobra, how's it going?" was a
greeting to which he responded with delight. One summer
in Arizona he killed a rattlesnake with his bare hands and
he wore the remains looped around his trousers.

Even the Russians were intrigued by face mask possibilities. A Moscow radio station had a competition for the most
original face mask that listeners could design for Tretiak,
their national team's brilliant goaltender, the one who Mark
Mulvoy had said felt goaltending was "ennobling." Hundreds of suggestions were sent in—most using the motif of
wolf or tiger heads. The listeners also used the opposite
approach: someone sent in a mask painted to the likeness of
a pretty girl, demure, with long eyelashes, a shy smile, the
sort of face (so the assumption was) that might cause even
the most hardened of Cossacks to take pause before zinging
a puck at it.

The most original idea—at least of those I read about—
was one which suggested that Tretiak affix a powerful electric beam to his mask to be used like a laser beam in a
science fiction epic.

All of this inspired me to a number of designs for my own
mask. I drew them clumsily on telephone pads. Some were
quirky—a chipmunk's face with small, apple cheeks, perky
and with a prominent pair of long teeth showing in the
middle of a sunny smile, bright blue eyes sparkling above;
some were meant to puzzle, such as one I designed that was
decorated with a large question mark; others were graphic
—a mask that read simply enough in red letters, NO!; yet
another was a psychedelic swirl that was supposed to make
anyone who gazed on it slightly dizzy.

The design I finally fixed upon seemed to combine all
these elements. I sent the mask to an artist friend of mine
in Rumson, New Jersey, with instructions to paint on it "a
large blue eye." My notion was that my own confidence

would be shored up by this image of being all-seeing, and that the forwards coming down the ice on attack would be transfixed by this great Cyclopean eye.

The artist's rendering, when I got it back, seemed graphic enough, but only—somewhat to my disappointment—when viewed from close to. The mask seemed pathetically small as I removed it from its wrappings; I experimented by putting the mask on the mantelpiece and stepping back . . . to find that the eye seemed to lose its hypnotic power beyond a range of about eight feet.

When my artist-friend called me up to see what I thought of his handicraft, I told him as much. He replied, "Well, you didn't exactly give me very much area to work with. The effect is not going to blaze across the ice like a Van Gogh flower."

"No," I agreed.

"You'll have to think of it as something for use at close quarters. If somebody gets really close to the goal, turn your face suddenly towards him and zap him with it."

"Absolutely."

So when the time came to leave for Fitchburg and the Bruins' training camp, I packed the mask in my suitcase along with the heavy goalie skates and some sweat suits, T-shirts, and four or five pairs of tennis socks. I packed a tin of Band-Aids for blisters. The face-mask eye stared up at me from the suitcase's contents. I dropped some T-shirts over it and zipped up the bag.

2

FITCHBURG is a small milltown about an hour-and-a-half's drive north of Boston. Driving in—at least by the route I took—one travels past the slope of a vast graveyard hill that overlooks the town. Its stones shine in the sun. I tried holding my breath as I drove by—that ancient boyhood ritual—but held up briefly in a small traffic congestion behind a truck full of chickens staring at me beadily through the slats of their crates, I could not do it: a large expulsive gasp and I murmured to myself that things would not go well.

I found my way to the Holiday Inn where the Bruins team was quartered. The rookies had been there a week. The veterans had come in the evening before. A group of young men wearing seersucker suits and ties were lounging around the entrance—somewhat elegant men at first glance, each with a plastic name tag affixed to his lapel which, as I approached close enough to read, bore the jolly announcement HI, I'M and the bearer's name written underneath in block letters. I thought fleetingly, Well, this is very genteel of the Bruins organization indeed—to make the newcomers feel so much at home!

But then I saw that the name plates identified the group as connected with the Simplex Corporation—executives, presumably, standing out in the afternoon sun on a coffee break.

My room was 136. I had been assigned a roommate. The Bruins organization thought it would help me in my research if I were settled in with another goalie. There had been guffaws in the background when they told me this over the phone. The rookie's name was Jim "Seaweed" Pettie. I was told he was quite a "number."

"Seaweed?" I asked.

Seaweed was not on hand when I unlocked the door and stepped into Room 136. The room, which was on the ground floor, seemed overcrowded with suitcases; a set of barbells rested against one wall. Although it was late afternoon, both beds were rumpled and unmade. I had been told at the front desk that there had been a second occupant, another Bruins rookie, but that he had been dropped from the roster earlier that morning and was being shipped out. The initials on a number of the bags read CWC. I hoped "CWC" would be leaving without any argument or rancor, at least not directed at me for being the one who was about to take over his bed.

The Gideon Bible lay open on a round table near the window. I could not resist glancing at it to see if perhaps it bore a message of significance to me at that time . . . one that might provide a better omen and would cancel out the consequences of my inability to hold my breath past the graveyard hill outside of town. I read: "He shall return no more to his house. Neither shall his place know him anymore."

Just then a figure appeared at the window, wrenched it open, and clambered in over the windowsill from the parking lot outside. He landed with a thump next to the table with the Gideon on it, and seeing me on the far side of the room, he called out my name, and announced himself as

"Seaweed." He came forward and we shook hands. He said he believed in shortcuts; that was why he had materialized through the window. "Welcome to the Union," he said, apparently in reference to my being considered a fellow goaltender. I grinned at him in gratitude.

I said I admired his abrupt entrance.

He laughed and said that he had learned it from Derek Sanderson who the year before was trying a comeback and was Seaweed's roommate during the training season. "He'd leap in through the window head-first and land on his stomach on the floor . . . a running start in the parking lot, through the flower bed, up and in. You'd hear a crash in there as he slid along the floor. One night we were coming back from an evening out in Fitchburg and after he'd parked the car he took his dive through the wrong window. I heard the crash and a kind of high nervous yell. Apparently there were three people in there, two of them watching television, and a third playing cards at a table. Sanderson passed out on the floor in a heap. I had to go around through the lobby, down a corridor, and get in their room to haul him out of there. The people were just in shock. Dumbfounded."

Physically, my roommate reminded me of a young, very agile version of Gene Wilder, the popeyed Hollywood character actor. He told me he was called "Seaweed" for the wild, stringy look of his hair during and after a game —a conditioning problem that was apparently hereditary since he informed me that his father's nickname was "Kelp." "Seaweed" was shortened to "Weed" by most of the Bruins, and that was what he told me the fans yelled in Rochester, New York, where he had played for the Americans, or Amerks as everyone called them, the Bruins' farm club. When he made a good save in the goal, the crowds would shout, "Weed! Weed!" He had also—he went on—

picked up the nickname "Mad Dog" . . . this for his aggressive play on the ice despite the limitations one would assume were imposed by being weighed down by all the
goaltending equipment. He told me he had been assessed
150 minutes during the preceding season at Rochester,
which is a record—he announced rather proudly—for goalies in the professional leagues; among other things he had
clambered up into the stands (he must have seemed, with
the bulk of his equipment on, like a gorilla on the loose)
to beat up a fan who was "chirping" at him.

"What's 'chirping'?" I asked.

"Mouthing off," he explained. "What you can't be in this
game is a candy-ass, which is a player who wants no part of
mucking it up."

"Mucking it up?"

"Protecting one's rights. Not letting anyone get advantage of you. Fighting . . ."

"Ahem," I said. "And even the goalies . . . ?"

"The great goaltenders have to muck it up to be respected," Seaweed said. "Tomorrow you'll be seeing Gerry
Cheevers. Players have such respect for him that you don't
ever find players standing in the crease with him. He belts
them in the ankles. He can break an ankle with his stick."

Seaweed leapt up and illustrated how this was done with
a wild swipe of his arm. I was to learn that this was a
common trait—to illustrate some technical aspect of goaltending with a physical pantomime . . . often a great leap
off the mattress that seemed to soar him up to the ceiling.
I knew I was in for an exhausting time. He was an incessant
talker. Hockey simply absorbed him. He told me that first
afternoon that he had read only one book completely
through, and that one many times—*The Jacques Plante Story*,
the goalie who had introduced the face mask. Most of his
family were involved in the hockey business—a Toronto

puck manufacturing concern called the Viceroy Rubber
Company. As Seaweed described it in his lively fashion:
"My mother makes pucks, my sister sells pucks, and I *eat*
pucks."

I told him that it was not a culinary habit I was looking
forward to.

"You may not have any choice," Seaweed said. "What
have you been doing to get ready?"

I told him about my evenings at the Skyrink in New York
and how the first time I stepped on the ice it was as if a
strawman had been flung out there. "I hadn't gone three
feet before I was down," I said. "So I went out there night
after night. I did a lot of reading, too," I went on. "I looked
at about fifty books on hockey."

"Have you read Plante's book?" Seaweed asked.

I told him I had. It had scared me. There was a part in
it in which I remembered Plante had said that being a
goaltender was like being shot at. He wrote that Bobby
Hull's slap shot would *kill* someone . . . it was said as simply
as that.

Seaweed said, "That shot of his would take your glove
off your hand and carry it back into the net with the puck
in it."

I believed it. I told Seaweed I was reminded of another
description I had read about Hull's shot by a goaltender
named Leo Binkley. "It starts off looking like a small pea
and then disappears altogether." I had another one, a
longer one—this by Gerry Desjardins, then with the Los
Angeles Kings. I had copied it in my notebook. I went and
got it out. "The one that scares me the most is Bobby Hull,"
I read aloud. "He scares every goalie, though he may lie
about it. He's built like a bull and skates like the wind and
he shoots from everywhere—the puck can be rolling on end
and he'll take a swipe at it—and his shot has been timed at

125 miles per hour and it's deadly accurate. He uses one of those curved sticks and the puck whistles in and curves and dances and sort of explodes on you. His shot is very heavy. If you can catch it, he can bruise you right through your glove. He hit me on my leg once and it was sore two months later. He can drive you into the nets with a shot . . . ."

My voice died away. It was this last image that left the most visual mental picture . . . the thought of being hit by a puck in the midsection and lifted up off my skates and jacknifed back into the folds of the net.

To ease my discomfiture, which was beginning to make me fidget, I tried to shift the focus away from my own problems; I asked Seaweed how he felt he was doing in the Bruins' camp.

Seaweed admitted that his chances of making the Bruins team were slim. Five goalies were in camp—the veteran Gerry Cheevers, Gilles Gilbert, and Ron Grahame who had come over from the recently defunct World Hockey Association, and the rookies—Dave Parro from Saskatoon and Seaweed himself.

"There's another one," I reminded him.

"Christ, yes, you!" Seaweed exclaimed in mock dismay, smacking himself in the center of his brow. "Six goalies in camp! That means a lot of 'riding the pines'—sitting on the bench."

"I won't mind that," I said. "I can take notes."

I mentioned that he didn't seem annoyed there were so many other goalies.

"Oh, no," he said. "We have to stick together. The Union!"

I asked if there was indeed that much distinction between the goalies and the rest of the team.

"Oh, absolutely," Seaweed said.

He went on to point out that Gerry Cheevers, the Bruins'

main-man goalie, never even shook hands with the opposing players when at the conclusion of a play-off series the
two teams lined up to exchange congratulatory handshakes,
never, ever—it was a contradiction to shake hands with
someone who has been firing a puck at you. But Cheevers
would skate past these lines of people, ignoring them pointedly, to shake the hand of the opposing goaltender. They
were both in the Union. Why, if a rival goalie got in a
slump, Cheevers would try to help him out of it! Goalies
stick together. They look after each other.

Seaweed had only played one game for the Bruins. The
year before he had been called up from the Rochester
Amerks when Cheevers left for home on an emergency
leave. At the pregame meeting, Don Cherry, the coach,
announced Seaweed's name as the starting goalie that night
against the Black Hawks . . . just at the end of the meeting
. . . and his Bruins teammates burst out laughing because
Seaweed's eyes popped so at the news. "I was sick immediately," Seaweed told me. "I got up from the meeting and
went into the crapper and got sick. Out on the ice I was sick
behind my mask the first time the Hawks came across the
red line. I was sick between the periods. I was sick after the
game."

"Did you manage . . . ?"

"Oh, I won the game 6–3," he said, using the personal
pronoun in the manner of a prize fight manager.

We began talking about how hockey players ever become involved in a position which gripped them with such
tension. Seaweed said, "Actually, it's usually the smallest
kid on the block who gets to be the goalie. In playing
ball-hockey in the summer he's the guy who's always made
to run down the street after the ball that's been shot wide.
He spends a lot of time under cars fishing for the ball. I
didn't much like running down the street, or getting dirty

from axle oil on my back, but I got to like the goaltending part of it. My grandfather would set me up in an alcove in the house and try to throw a baseball past me."

It is almost impossible to find goaltenders who willingly took on the position at the start of their hockey careers. Glenn Hall, often announced by the Chicago public address announcer as "Mister Goalie," had become a goalie at the advanced age of thirteen in his home town of Humboldt, Saskatchewan, because just before a pick-up game no one else on the team would volunteer; the opposing players skated around, jeering, waiting for someone to make up his mind. Hall finally shrugged and went in—"between the pipes," which was one of Seaweed's phrases for being in goal—because he realized that there was not going to be a game if he didn't.

Once in, the player seemed stuck there for good. I told Seaweed that in my reading I had found only one player, Harry "Rat" Westwick, who had moved from being a goaltender out to the forward position. He performed at the turn of the century with the Ottawa Silver Seven and as a forward averaged better than a goal a game.

"Rat?" commented Seaweed. "Yeah. He was no member of the Union to be doing a thing like that."

There were, however, a number of interesting examples of the *reverse*—forwards and defensemen who had abruptly been pressed into service as goalies. What transpired, however quick they were with skates and their hands, was predictable and disastrous. A defenseman named Harry Mummery, who played for the Quebec Bulldogs in the 1920s, was ordered into the nets—all the regular goalies had been put out of action—where he immediately had eleven goals scored on him by the Ottawa Senators. Curiously, he rather enjoyed his evening at that position—more likely because of his gargantuan eating habits which diminished his effectiveness anywhere on the ice *except* in the goal: he weighed 250 pounds and was known to cook meals, big steaks, down in the ice rink furnace room.

One of the most famous examples of a goalie being relieved by a stranger to the position was Lester Patrick's feat when he was the coach of the New York Rangers. His goalie, Lorne Chabot, had been carried off with an eye injury. No replacements were available in those days—it was just assumed that a goalie would spit out a tooth or clap a hand over an eye and yell "Hey!" and then go on. Patrick put himself in. He is supposed to have called out to his people as he skated lumpily to his position, "Check as you have never checked before, fellows, and protect an old man."

The Rangers took a 1–0 lead into the third period, but Montreal—its city's team was the Maroons then—scored a tying goal and the game went into overtime. Frank Boucher, a member of the Rangers' famous "A Line" with Bill and Bun Cook—who in the off-season was a member of the Royal Canadian Mounted Police—scored at 5:07 of the overtime. Patrick, his jaw agape, skated off the ice, scarcely believing what he had been able to accomplish.

"They would have given him the standing 'O,' that's for sure," Seaweed said.

"The what?"

"The big 'O.' The Ovation. That's what we're all working for out here—the standing 'O.' "

I suddenly thought to ask about the mysterious second roomate—the player with the initials CWC whose gear, including the barbells presumably, was stored along the wall.

" 'O' for 'Out.' He's gone," Seaweed said. He went over to one of the suitcases. "Try lifting this thing."

I could barely budge it off the floor.

"It's full of barbells and weight-lifting material. Irons."
Seaweed explained. "They belong to Wild Bill Frazier."

"Wild Bill Frazier?"

Seaweed said that Frazier had been dropped by the
Bruins—"gassed" was the expression he used—just the day
before.

"Why is all this luggage still here?" I asked.

"Wild Bill is a strange guy," Seaweed said. "He may
have just gone off and left the stuff for good. I mean there's
nothing in those bags but a lot of iron."

"What about the initials—CWC?"

Seaweed shrugged. "Maybe he borrowed those suitcases
from his girlfriend. Or an aunt. But I've never seen anything in them but weight-lifting equipment. He arrived
with one pair of bluejeans, a T-shirt, and two tons of iron
to pump . . . building himself up so he could fight."

Seaweed went on to say that Frazier's hope of making the
squad was actually based almost entirely on his willingness
to mix it up and slug people—what hockey people called a
"goon." So he worked with those barbells all day and night
when he wasn't at practice. He'd wake him up in the middle
of the night: "Hey, Seaweed, do you think I should start a
brawl at tomorrow's practice?"

Seaweed said he would stir from his sleep and suggest
that perhaps Frazier should wait until the Bruins played
another team. "That'd be a good time to do it."

"But, Seaweed," Frazier had replied. "It might be too
late. I could be gone before I can show the coach that I can
really stick people."

Seaweed said he could hear the bedsprings squeak as
Wild Bill worked the barbells. "I don't think that guy ever
slept," he told me, "what with building up his strength and
thinking about whether he was going to bust someone. He
was a true goon, which is a guy who will go."

"How many goons are there on the Bruins?" I wanted
to know.

"During the exhibition season there are a lot of them on
every team," Seaweed said, "racing around and trying to
make an impression. Goalies like us have to look out for
them, because they're wild, and they'll put it up in the top
drawer, shoot up on the roof a lot."

"Up on the roof . . ."

"They'll throw the puck in high and bust you in the
melon, like as not."

Seaweed was an expert at the lingo. That first day I
learned that the head was not only the "melon" but also the
"puss," the "pumpkin," the "coconut."

"The dumb guys on a club," Seaweed continued, "are
called 'cement-heads.' You don't find too many of them in
hockey, but we had one on our club in Rochester. He's
called 'Portland.' "

"Does he mind?" I asked.

"No, because it's true," Seaweed said. "And besides I'm
not sure he's yet made the connection between 'Portland'
and 'cement.' "

The worst put-down, far worse than being called a "ce-
ment-head" apparently, was to say of someone: "He's got
no seeds."

"That's like handing a guy a white feather," Seaweed
said.

"Oh yes."

"Nothing worse than that."

"I see."

"What's the goal called?" I asked, changing the subject.

Seaweed said that old-time goalies referred to "being in
the barrel," but these days no self-respecting goaltender
would say such a thing. It was a demeaning phrase apparently—the connotation being a fish in a barrel, or in a barrel

going over Niagara Falls, or a clown in a circus barrel.

Seaweed was adamant about it. "A goalie might say he was 'going between the pipes' or 'in the cell' but he would never say he was going in the barrel."

"But it would be accurate."

"Oh yes," he admitted. "Damn right. Yes. You'll see. Tomorrow. You'll see in the first practice."

I asked, "What's the worst time a goalie ever had in the nets?"

Seaweed said he had heard of a goalie named Lorne Anderson, who was a third-string goaltender for the Rangers in the early fifties. He knew about it because he had established a rather dubious record. In a game against the Chicago Black Hawks, Bill Mosienko of Chicago's famous Pony Line had got three shots past Anderson in 21 seconds!

"Mosienko said about it, "I caught lightning in a beer bottle.' "

"What about Anderson?" I asked. "What happened to him?"

"I believe that was his last game in the NHL. Maybe not too surprising."

I went over to my suitcase and took out the face mask painted like a blue eye. "Do you think this is going to help?" I asked.

"What is this?" Seaweed said, coming over to peer at it.

"I thought I'd get something painted on the mask that'll really shake them up."

Seaweed took the mask and turned it in his hand slowly. "Does it fit?"

I told him it did.

"What's this?"

"An eye."

After a while, Seaweed said: "It looks like a target. It's not a good idea. Some goon is sure to wing a shot off it.

Your melon isn't going to feel so good." He went on to say that he felt the safest mask for me was the style developed by the Russians, the "wire-cage" model which looked like a catcher's mask. He was sure the Bruins' equipment manager would be able to find me one. "But this thing? No. No. I'd repack it. You skate out onto the ice with this thing on and there'll be bets to see who's the first to hit the bullseye!"

3

T H E next morning Seaweed and I drove through Fitchburg to the Wallace Indoor Rink on the other side of town where the Bruins for some years have had their preseason headquarters. I left my face mask with the blue eye back in the motel room. My notion of decorating my mask was going by the boards. The Russian-style mask with its gratelike front—which Seaweed said I would be getting —does not allow much in the way of decoration . . . any more than one could paint a design on a row of prison cell bars. The forehead part of the mask has a small area on which something might be done, but usually the manufacturer utilizes the space to advertise his name. The word "Cooper"—to pick a helmet maker at random—does not exactly strike terror in the heart of any skater who happens to glance up and read it.

The weather was bad. I had gone out for supper with Seaweed the night before, and after a long night of listening to him talk about hockey, the tick of the windshield wipers had a lulling, soothing effect, so that despite my fears as to what was coming, I walked into the Bruins' locker room yawning mightily.

I was shown to a secondary locker room; almost all of us in there were rookies. Seaweed called it the "lepers' room."

Occasionally, the veterans would peek in through the door. I recognized a number of them. I had studied their faces in the game programs of the preceding season—Wayne Cashman, Terry O'Reilly, who they called the Tasmanian Devil, Rick Smith, Peter McNab, and Bobby Schmautz—"that's 'Doctor Hook,' " the awed rookie next to me whispered. I felt myself the object of their quick scrutiny. They had heard I was joining up, so they looked around the corner of the lepers' room door to assess this odd specimen who would be one of them for a while. It did not improve my sense of well-being.

That first day the other goalies must have gathered beforehand and decided that they were going to scare the wits out of me. As soon as I had settled onto the bench in front of the locker stall to which I had been assigned, Gerry Cheevers came up to introduce himself and show me his famous face mask—crisscrossed with the stitch marks painted on where the pucks over the years had busted him in the "melon"—as Seaweed would have said. "Look at this one—across the nose," Cheevers pointed out. "I got hit in St. Louis, and if I hadn't been wearing the mask, I'd be dead. In fact, even with the mask I thought I was gone."

Gilles Gilbert, whose young, angel-face features suggested perhaps he had escaped the ravages of the puck, told me that quite to the contrary: in three weeks' time playing for the Three Rivers (Quebec) junior team he had lost all his top teeth when a defenseman ducked under a shot fired unseen from the point (Gilles had tossed aside his face mask because the crowd had started booing a pair of breakaway goals scored against him), all his bottom teeth two weeks later, and a week subsequent to that he had turned his head and lost part of his ear to a puck. He saw the piece lying on the ice and fell over in a faint. "That was the first time my parents ever saw me play," he told me.

Don Cherry, the Boston coach, saw me looking uncom-
fortable. He came over—a small, cheerful man with a cocki-
ness of manner and stature that afterwards always made me
remember he had been the drummer in a marching bagpipe
band. Everyone called him "Grapes." He sat down on the
bench next to me. "You'll be O.K. I mean, you're going
to live," he said. "I've never seen a goalie get a serious
injury—even before the time of the masks. People say that
in the premask times the goalies stood up more, so their
faces would be up above the goal mouth, but Terry Sawchuk, he'd hang his bare face two or three feet off the ice
so's he could see through the screens. Nothing happened
to him on the ice. He died after wrestling with a player, Ron
Stewart, out on a lawn, at his house in New York. Or take
the goalie, Bobby Perreault, I once played with—a little
short guy, 5'6", pot-bellied and bald, who never wore a
mask, and hardly any protection at all. Nothing bothered
him. I remember he got hit real bad once in the melon, just
an awful thing to see, and I skated up to him and called out,
'Bobby, Bobby, you all right?' He answered, 'I'm all right.
How's the *crowd* taking it?' "

Cherry shifted on the bench. "Oh, he was a tough one.
But the biggest trouble he ever had was the afternoon he
lost Dick Irvin's pigeons. Irvin was the Montreal coach, but
his great love was not the Canadiens but his pigeons; he had
a real penchant for collecting them. This one time Irvin
bought a whole mess of them, out on a road trip, and
Perreault was assigned to guard them; somehow he got
fooling around with the cage and the pigeons began to get
out. You'd think a goalie with all those quick reflexes, and
the agility and everything, would be able to handle a bunch
of pigeons, but maybe they were a big, fresh bunch, and
what with the flapping and all, feathers flying around—I
think they were on a railroad station platform—Perreault

panicked, and they all got away. Irvin went crazy. Maybe he thought Perreault's reflexes were beginning to go. What happened was that Perreault disappeared into the minors. I saw him once. 'You all right?' I ask him. 'Oh, I'm all right. No luck,' he tells me. He didn't mind where he was or what happened to him. But I always reckoned he wanted to get out of the game. That was a strange way to slide out, wasn't it?—letting those pigeons out of the cage. So there you are," Cherry concluded mysteriously. "You haven't got anything to worry about."

I thanked him. I said I thought he had made me feel much better. I went into the training room to get my ankles taped. I was the only player who did. Jim Kausek, the trainer, looked at my thin, cranelike structure. "You are not what usually comes and sits on this rubbing table," he said. "I get mesomorphs. Muscular, shortish legs, and big hams. Huge upper arms and torso strength. If I may say, you haven't got much heft in the upper torso. Bones."

"I'm afraid you've got yourself the quintessential ectomorph."

"Very rare around here," he said. He said he hadn't taped an ankle for years. If I hadn't come along he probably would have forgotten how to do it. The ankle was never a professional hockey player's worry. The great anxiety was the knee. That was the area to which the greatest stress was transferred. It was the problem area for hockey players as it was in so many other sports. The knee. That was what happened to Bobby Orr. A bag of handkerchiefs. That was what his knee looked like. He couldn't get in on a gentleman's tennis game with that knee—one of the greatest athletes who ever lived.

After being taped, it usually took me fifteen minutes or so to prepare myself for the ice. But that first day, with the other goalies, headed by Seaweed, and the equipment man-

ager crowding around me to show me what to do—rather
like squires preparing a French knight for the field at Agin-
court—I struggled with the equipment for over half an
hour. The order of dress was important. If you left something out of the proper sequence, some kind of pad, for
instance, then you had to undress back down to the stage
when it was supposed to have gone on.

First, the athletic supporter. Then, a long white union
suit. All the players wore them: before a game they lounged
around the locker room in them like a restless collection of
out-sized rabbits. Or big gnomes wearing Doctor Dentons.
Some of the players cut the pants leg off at the knees. Mine
were full-length. Then a pair of thick socks. Next, the
goalie's protective cup—the large mold made of a hard
plastic substance which gives off a dull thud when knocked
with a fist. When a puck hits it, it gives off a high bong. It
was a sound—according to Seaweed—referred to as "ringing the berries." He went on to say that to be hit in the
berries by a hard shot—a "stinger" he called it—resulted in
a pain like "taking your top lip and folding it back over your
head."

"Oh yes," I said.

Many goalies stuffed newspapers or cotton into the protective cup, but Seaweed felt this was psychological as much
as anything.

"It doesn't help?" I asked.

Seaweed replied that he doubted a goalie had gone out
there in the nets to test ("Can you imagine the guy angling
his body so he'd be hit in the berries by the puck?")
whether it was less painful "with" or "without" but certainly his impression was that a "stinger" would hurt no
matter what.

"Naturally."

After adjusting the protective cup (in my case, despite

my roommate's skepticism I subsequently stuffed it with
large sections of the Fitchburg *Herald*) the goalie slips on
the garter belt, with its clips along the base to hold up the
heavy wool stockings with the yellow and black Bruins
markings. Then, the hockey pants—stiff as cardboard, so
that stepping into them was like pulling a pair of barrels up
around the waist. Next, the skates—special goalie's skates
with toe and ankle protectors, and blades designed to keep
a puck from sliding through. The blades were kept comparatively dull, so that a goalie could slide laterally across
the ice in the crease without being brought up short by the
sharpness of his skates' edges.

After the skates come the goalie's big leg pads, cumbersome, the thickness of a mattress, with two straps at the
bottom that hitch the pads to the skates, and eight more up
the back. The procedure for getting them on was to kneel
on the pads on the locker room floor and crane over one's
shoulder while fumbling to attach the straps.

Once done, the goalie rears up and pummels the pads
and pushes them around to get them adjusted to the legs
properly. The pads have a compartment-like hollow that
runs down their length into which some goalies stuff maga-
zines for cushioning. I kept a notebook in the compartment
of my left-leg pad, along with a felt-tipped pen, to remind
myself of my reportorial obligations; Seaweed suggested
that I keep a whiskey flask in there—to have a swig for
"courage" from time to time.

After setting the pads as comfortably as possible, the
goalie puts on the following: a pair of knee pads, a chest
protector like a baseball catcher's with clips that fasten
around the back, a pair of arm protectors as stiff as stove
pipes, and a small bib around the neck that is supposed to
keep the Adam's apple from being caved in.

"It'll help," Don Cherry said, who had given me the bib.

"But remember there is no such thing as 'painless' goal-tending. If they could get enough padding to assure against any type of bruise, you'd have to be swung into position with a small derrick."

While getting strapped in with all this paraphernalia, it crossed my mind that Paul Cannell, an English soccer forward who once played for the Memphis Rogues soccer team, had a reputation for dropping his shorts and showing his backside to protest referees' calls against him. In hockey it would take about ten minutes to get that gesture under-way—considering the shoulder pads, the suspenders to snap off the shoulders, skinning off the jersey to get at them, and so forth, so that by the time the backside was in view every-one would have forgotten the *reason* for the gesture.

I asked the proper procedure for ragging an official.

"You thinking of doing that?" Cheevers asked.

"Heavens, no!" I said. "Just curious."

The equipment being parceled out to me was worn and second-hand and from the start I noticed that a strange ripe-cheese odor drifted off some of the items—partly acrid, which was doubtless from the sweat that no amount of steam laundering could erase; but there was something else: the smell of funk, perhaps—at least that is what I took it to be—that would exude from the long terrifying exertions required of goaltending . . . a curious, penetrating odor— a shower never seemed to rid me of it completely—that seemed caught permanently in some corner of the nostrils; a whiff of it would arrive suddenly in my consciousness, weeks later, while riding in a bus, and I would think, Oh, I'm stuck with this forever, and there are people, especially up in Canada, who recognize this odd aroma, and the man on the seat opposite is going to nudge his neighbor and remark, "Hey, Ed, that's a goalie sitting there."

It was an odd odor. But then one never knew how it

affected others. I reminded myself that H. G. Wells felt that
his enormous success with women was attributable to his
natural body scent of violets.

Not that this odor was violet! Sometimes the whiff was
so strong that I thought I had been the victim of a practical
joke—that the Bruins had dosed my equipment with a mysterious scent which they pretended not to notice, and that
in fact, on the bench, or out on the town with them after
practice, I was floating among the citizens of Fitchburg, and
through their taverns, in a potent, odoriferous haze. I became conditioned to it. On the ice, the game jersey with the
yellow-spoked wheel, for the Hub, had a strong, pleasant
laundered smell which did much to cut the pungency of
what was underneath.

The gloves. The blocking glove, often called the "stick
glove," or "backhand glove," went on the hand that carried
the stick (in my case, the right), a glove backed with a thick
rectangular board pocked with air holes. It was used as a
kind of shield (the blocker) to deflect shots coming in high
on the goalie's stick side. On the other hand went the huge
"catching" or "trapper" mitt, a vast one, with a long sleeve
reaching almost to the elbow so—I was informed succinctly
—"you won't get your wrists and lower arm bones broken." The glove part was much more malleable than I had
imagined, so that I could flap the leather jaws open and shut
with a big slapping sound. Seaweed told me that it was
important to catch the puck in the lower portions of the
glove, because, as I would find out, there was no padding
to protect the hand itself, and if the puck came in high in
the glove and smacked the palm, the pain would soar up the
arm and shatter the frame of the body like a heavy calibre
gunshot wound.

The masks. Sure enough. The equipment manager was
able to supply me with the wire-cage model Seaweed had

recommended. Apparently it was developed by Vladislav Tretiak himself and its catcher's mask lines are coming increasingly into vogue in the league. The equipment manager told me it would not have been wise to wear a face-fitting mask no matter what I was going to paint on it. It was crazy to buy one over the counter. The only safe mask of that type—at least one which would stand up to an NHL slap shot—was one which had been form-fitted—a lengthy process which involved wrapping the goaltender's face like a mummy's to make a plaster of Paris mold from which the fiber glass mask could be fashioned.

The great expert at making masks and goalie's equipment was Frank Kenesky, from the Kenesky dynasty which had been in the business of keeping goaltenders sound of limb since Pop Kenesky, a tobacco-chewing harness maker from Hamilton, Ontario, started the company at the turn of the century. One of his first innovations was a leg pad that stuck stiffly out at the sides—quite a departure from the cricket-pad wraparound protection that the goaltenders wore in the early 1900s. Pop Kenesky died in 1975 at the age of ninety-eight, having hand-made pads for almost every goaltender in professional hockey—300 pairs a year, stuffed with deer hair, at about $140 a set, one of which, ordered by Earl Robertson of the New York Americans, was required to have two rabbit's feet built into it.

Kenesky's hands had undoubtedly worked on the rather elderly pair that encompassed my legs, and which, when I stood up, gave me the sensation of being settled permanently into place, like a heavy piece of garden sculpture. When a goalie has got all of his equipment on he is weighed down by about thirty-five pounds. However graceful the goaltender may turn out to be on the ice, he moves from the locker room across the rubber mattings for the rink with the ponderous gait of a dowager coming down a church aisle.

My own approach to the ice was even more tentative. I put one skate slowly in front of the other. I kept close to the wall of the locker room to use it to prop myself up in case I started to topple. I stepped out into the corridor to the rink side. Seaweed clumped along behind me. The door in the boards with its big iron hasp was swung ajar. I put one skate out on the ice, pushed off with the other, and moved out onto the vast expanse where the Bruins circled.

Some of them were waiting for me . . . to make sure that I would remember my entrance into their world. Just as I took my first stride on the ice, I was startled by a concussive bang on the protective glass that surrounds the rink—a ringing *ccc-rack!* at head level just off to one side. I was concentrating so hard on remaining upright that I never bothered to turn to see what it was that had made such a noise. Later, I learned that Dave Forbes, one of the Bruins forwards, seeing me step on the ice, felt that I should be greeted in some way—introduced to the ways of the National Hockey League—and he fired a puck high up on the protective glass, just two or three feet down the line from my head. *Ccc-rack!*

Behind the glass Don Cherry happened to be standing with a friend of his who had stopped by to watch the practice. As they watched the Bruins handle the puck, Cherry was remarking how accurate professional hockey players were with their shots—they knew exactly where they were putting the puck . . . and it was just then that Forbes fired his shot past my head. Cherry's friend paled. "My God, Grapes, did you see that?"

"What?" Cherry had missed seeing it.

"Well, one of your Bruins just missed that goalie's head!

Wildest shot I ever saw." He pointed at the spot on the glass
where the puck had hit. "It only missed the goalie by a foot.
Look, it's even affected him. Look how he's skating out
there."

Cherry looked over. "Oh, *that* goalie."

"What's wrong with him?"

Cherry told me later that he had kidded his friend. He
said that I was a hot prospect from Quebec somewhere who
didn't look like much, sort of slow and clumsy, but who
thrived and was an absolute whiz only under the severest
competition. The rest of the time I dogged it.

The friend looked at my maidenly progress across the ice
and said, "Grapes, the guy doesn't give me good vibes."

T H E practices were much simpler than I imagined they
would be. There was no instruction, no plays diagrammed
on a blackboard, indeed hardly any communication between the coach (usually just Don Cherry or his assistant on
the ice) and his players except that a whistle would blow
from time to time and we would be told what procedure to
do next.

The practice started with the players wheeling the long
length of the ice for five minutes or so, alternately shifting
into high gear and then slacking off at the coach's whistle;
my fellow goalies, though the bulk of their pads forced a
more oblique skating stroke, seemed to clip along at speeds
just a touch under the others'. My own speed was about half
of theirs, a decorous ten knots or so until at the whistle
indicating that we should speed up I would increase my
pace and come down the stretch at twelve knots—I kept
thinking of myself as a kind of houseboat amongst them—
before setting the outside leg and starting the slow stem
turn around the back of the cage. The Bruins sailed by.

Occasionally a stick would reach out to tap me on the pads, and I would wobble alarmingly.

Periodically, Coach Cherry would blow his whistle and yell at us to skate backwards . . . which the Bruins could do as fast as they went forward, the skates roaring *(slur-slur-slur)* as the edges hit the ice in the quick S-motions of the skater in reverse. My own speed backwards was in the neighborhood of two knots at the most, done gingerly, without much body motion, so that from afar it must have seemed that what was moving me was a zephyr. I always kept close to the boards.

The warm-ups were followed by a series of drills—various combinations of offense against the defense—for fifteen minutes or so, and then the scrimmaging would begin. That was Cherry's principle—to get the squads scrimmaging as soon as possible. He was a disciple of Montreal's Toe Blake. He told me: "Blake's idea was, 'Don't get the game confusing.' He'd skate his squads twice around the rink one way, twice the other, then drop the puck and let them scrimmage."

The scrimmages were spirited. From the bench the players leaned over the boards and banged them with their sticks when one of their squad-mates made a good play. Seaweed sat next to me. When one of the opposing squad missed a check and banged into the boards near our bench, he would call out, "Ah, you couldn't check a coat!" It was the chatter he referred to as "chirping," and it was constant background to the practices, like the outcry of a jay in the autumn woods. There were very few face-offs. When the puck was confined by the boards, the players inching it laboriously along, the coaches would call out, "Work it out of there, work it out!" rather than blowing the whistle and calling for a face-off.

The lines went out over the boards on an average of

every ninety seconds. After almost two minutes of hard
skating in a scrimmage, the coaches reckon that an edge to
the player's speed and quickness has gone sufficiently to
require a replacement. It is even less in a game. The new
line hops over. It takes about thirty seconds for the player
to sit on the bench and puff and get a plastic water bottle
to squirt a stream onto the roof of his mouth to get his
breath back and be considered capable for another turn out
on the ice.

There was almost no stopping of play during the scrimmages to explain, say, tactics. "Hockey is not complicated,"
Don Cherry told me later. "When Bobby Schmautz joined
the team in Philly—we'd picked him up for $2,000 after he
was about to be waived through the league—I showed him
every play we had . . . drawing them out on a lunch counter
napkin in five minutes."

Seated with the others on the bench, I kept wondering
when I was going to be inserted into the action. I knew the
moment was going to come, of course, dreading it, and I
kept scribbling in my notebook as if to convince the coaches
if they glanced over that I was hard at work, ruminating,
putting down important observations, and that it would be
criminal for them to interrupt my train of thought. But
finally, a whistle would blow, and I'd look up to notice
Cheevers from the goal, or perhaps it was Seaweed, or
Gilbert, or Parro—it was hard to tell behind the white
masks they all wore, quite inhuman, like the bland faces of
barn owls, I often thought—nodding in my direction, motioning at me with their big gloves to come out onto the ice
and relieve them. I would look to see if it wasn't someone
else they wanted, but it wasn't, of course.

Don Cherry would call out my name and with a slight
sigh I would tuck the notebook away in the pads along with
the felt pen attached, settle the big glove onto my left hand,

grab the big goaltender's stick with the other, rise, and shuffle past the knees of my teammates ("Excuse me, excuse me") toward the gatelike door in the boards for my entry onto the ice. The voyage to the distant nets always seemed a long one. I skated it in a style as nonchalant as I could muster. Some of the Bruins as I cruised by them called out encouragement. I could hear Seaweed's piping voice from the bench: "Shut 'em down, roomie!" banging his stick against the boards. Halfway to the nets I would set my skates so that my momentum would carry me just to the mouth of the goal; it was essential not to arrive at the net with any velocity, because my inability to stop sharply would have required putting out my arms to stop myself against the top bar of the cage and perhaps (the indignity of them all!) with enough force to dislodge the cage from its underpinnings and slide with it into the backboards. So it was important to gauge things so that one *eased* into the goal mouth; there one could revolve slowly, and then face out into that vast expanse of ice: that was always the first impression—how interminable and surreal that vista was— a few people standing around in it like statuary in a winter landscape, until of course the whistle blew, the puck was dropped, at which point things became very hectic.

At first, Cheevers stood off to one side of the goal to advise . . . showing me how to drift out to cut down the angle as the wings came down the ice. "Come out, come out," he would call, because my tendency was to huddle inside the cage and peer out like a hedgehog. He wanted me at the top of the crease. He'd shout, "Keep your stick on the ice!" or often, just to remind me, "Stand up! Stand up!" knowing that if I toppled over, I was as useless, thrashing about, as a turtle on its back.

Inevitably, Cheevers would skate off after a while and let me fend for myself. If I made a save, the Bruins would lean

out from the bench and slam their hockey sticks along the
boards; a goal was greeted with silence, though I could hear
the laughter rise from the spectators in the stands. After
every score I would groan inside my mask and look for
relief, staring pointedly at the bench in the hope I would
see one of the regular goalies reach for his mask and his
stick. As I would stand there, looking out beseechingly, the
defensemen would rummage in the nets behind me, fishing
in there for the puck. Those were Seaweed's instructions—
never to bother with the puck . . . the established procedure
for the Union was to stand looking fixedly ahead, and let
other people deal with the damning evidence behind. Even
in the shooting drills I noticed that Seaweed never touched
the pucks collecting by the dozens in the back of the net.

I went through some frightening indignities. That first
day, the ultimate occurred when a puck emerged from a
melee at the blue line and came floating down the ice toward me, not so much a shot as a push, moving along at
about the speed that a dog trots; it was what Terry Sawchuk
apparently called a "softie." I glared at it; my intent was to
sweep it up into the corner for the defensemen to pick up,
but as I swiped at it, I lifted the stick just enough for the
puck to slide underneath, between my skates, and into the
goal. I even had time to turn and see the puck sliding slowly
across the red line at the goal mouth; I could have read the
lettering on the puck as it went in; it moved with barely
enough momentum to reach the back of the net.

I subsequently wrote in my goalie's pad notebook "utterly devastated." The laughter had echoed around the
rink; this time the players had chimed in. They could not
contain themselves.

Back on the bench I expected a barrage of joshing, but
the Bruins were surprisingly gentle. Sometimes they were
solicitous: "Well, they say Sawchuk couldn't handle a shot

high on the short side either." Some of them, surely to
lighten my embarrassment, leaned down the line to describe horrors that had happened to them. One of the defensemen, Darryl Edestrand, told me that once, in the process of trying to clear the puck from the front of the goal
and shoot it into the corners, he had turned and fired it
crisply into the corner of his own net! On his part, Gilles
Gilbert described gloving a puck and while trying to shake
it out onto the ice having it stick in the webbing and tumble
out backwards through the goal face!

"That's nothing." It was Cheevers from down the line.
He said that Bernie Parent had been scored on from *center
ice*—a shot by Barry Gibbs of the North Stars who was
probably trying to flip the puck into the zone and was as
surprised as anyone, certainly Parent, when the shot went
in.

"What about you, Cheesie? Haven't you got one to tell
him?"

Cheevers shrugged. He remembered the Forum in
Montreal when Terry Harper ("a good player, always in
the middle of things, but who never had any sort of shot,
nothing like a cannon at all, who got maybe one goal a
year") threw a shot that missed the net by eight feet and
caromed straight out off the boards. "I went out to control
it," Cheevers said. "The puck sideswiped off my skates and
went at a diagonal into the goal. It went in like I'd kicked
it in."

All this banter got me feeling better, indeed grinning
smugly at anyone who could make such ridiculous errors.
I would sit there, the sweat cooling, and the shame would
drift away. I would reach into my leg pad for the notebook.
It was all right for a time.

But then sooner or later someone would tap me on the
shoulder. "You're wanted. Look!" and I would see who-

ever was in goal waving me on. I would mumble, the sweat already beginning to break out, and start shuffling for the gate.

Sometimes after a stint in the goal I would skate out and join Don Cherry standing at midice over by the boards. He often seemed to me to be in need of company; I very rarely heard him call out instructions or criticisms. The play seemed to swirl past him without any orchestration on his part . . . as if the mechanism worked on its own. The lines hopped over the boards without any apparent signal. . . .

"How do they do that, Grapes?" I asked him as we stood together. "How do the players know when to change lines?"

"The order is pretty much determined beforehand," Cherry said. "In a game I'm more involved. I'll yell out, 'Ratelle's line up next!' Then out on the ice Peter McNab will raise his stick, give some sort of sign, and as he skates for the bench, I'll call out 'Up!' What effects the change is not so much tactics as running out of steam. In the old days —the fifties, say—the lines could stay out for as long as two or three minutes; the play was much slower then; they meandered around. These days in a game they're out there skating at absolutely full throttle; you can only do that for thirty or forty seconds."

"Does a player ever refuse to come off when he's supposed to?"

Cherry said, "Phil Esposito hated to come off, and many times he wouldn't. Andy Savard, who was supposed to come in for him, would be left dangling there on the boards, one leg over, waiting. He waited there so often that the guys used to joke that his position astride the boards, half over, half not, was going to make him sterile!"

Down in one of the goals I had the sense that Pettie or someone was waving me in. I looked away . . . like a

schoolboy who avoids the master's eyes in the hope he
won't be called on. Cherry caught me at it.

"You don't seem to have much of that Esposito spirit,"
he said with a grin.

I said, "I truly don't mind resting . . . standing out here
with you . . . or riding the pines. It allows me to soak up
atmosphere."

T H E scrimmage took up the bulk of the practice, which
lasted about an hour and a half. When the scrimmage was
whistled over, the squad lined up along the boards for ten
minutes or so of wind sprints before heading for the locker
room—racing across the width of the rink and back. I skated
with the goaltenders, inevitably in their wake after three or
four strides. Often, unable to commit myself to setting my
skates laterally in the traditional form to stop, I would run
full tilt into the boards, my hands outstretched to buffer
against the collision, my posture that of a horror-movie
mummy feeling its way down a corridor. Thus brought to
an abrupt stop, I could turn myself around to set off again.
As one of the Bruins remarked, I was the only player he had
ever seen in an NHL uniform who checked *himself* into the
boards.

The sprints were exhausting, especially tacked on to the
end of the scrimmage . . . enough, I would have thought,
to send the players drifting wearily and slowly off to the
locker room when Cherry finally blew his whistle to end the
practice. But to my surprise most of the players continued
to linger on the ice: they practiced their shots, their passing;
often they seemed to skate about haphazardly if just for the
pleasure of it; sometimes, two of them would pair off and
begin bear wrestling each other, reaching over each others'
shoulders to try to unbutton the suspenders and bring the

shirt up over the other's head, practicing what they hoped to do in a real fight—"turn out the lights on him" as Seaweed described it to me.

They made bets on their skills. When Seaweed got in the goal, Wayne Cashman bet him—half-kidding—two hundred dollars for every one of five penalty shots he could get by him . . . two hundred for each he scored, two hundred to Seaweed for each one he stopped. Seaweed said, "Two hundred is a lot," thinking the amount was the total for all five. Cashman said, "You can only lose a grand." Seaweed whistled sharply and said, "I'll play for a pitcher of beer."

He must have been relieved those were the terms because he lost four pitchers of beer, and almost a fifth when Cashman's fifth shot hit the post. "Whew!" Seaweed called to me as he stripped off his mask and skated out of the goal mouth.

They got me back in the goal and made me practice. They whooped to warn me a shot was coming. Cashman wanted to do some penalty-shot wagering, offering big odds, but I kept shaking my head until he skated off. Seaweed came over and demonstrated some of the various postures the goaltender could assume: the half-split, the butterfly drop, the double-leg slide. "Then, of course, there's the full-split."

He showed me.

"Yes," I said. "Very impressive. It's like the gymnast's split on the high beam."

"Try it."

"Seaweed, I don't think I can get up from it."

"Go on."

"If I happened to get into that position with the ice slightly sticky, I'd be glued there forever."

"Go ahead."

"Please."

I finally did it, afterwards hauling myself up by grabbing the top bar of the cage.

"You have a point," Seaweed said after my demonstration. "I'd only use it in extreme situations. Next . . . you must get over the habit of looking back to see where you are. You do that a lot. You keep turning your head like an owl. Cardinal rule. Always face to the front."

"Well, that's to check where I am in relation to the goal," I said. "I mean suppose I find I'm not in front of it."

I explained a vision I had of myself crouched, prepared, stick properly squared to the ice, grimly facing forward, and unaware that the goal itself was not directly behind me, but off on the diagonal, completely unprotected.

Seaweed reassured me. "You can glide backwards and feel the top bar against your back. Or reach back with your stick and feel for the sides. But don't look back unless play has stopped. What you'll find back there if you look is the puck in the back of the net."

Always the kidding went on. The remarks. Sometimes one of the Bruins, usually a veteran, would come at me full tilt and then brake sharply, in front of the net, sending up a fine spray of ice shavings off the sides of his skates which would sift in a heavy, prickling cloud-shower through the mesh of my mask. It was actually quite a soothing, if startling sensation—to feel the cool wash of ice droplets settle in among the beads of perspiration. Once, Bobby Schmautz came sweeping by and did it, such a violent spray of ice shavings sweeping up that I lost my balance; my skates flew out in front of me and I half-toppled back into the net, caught briefly in there, struggling around like a bird in a fishnet. I extricated myself and skated out to where Don Cherry was standing at midice.

"I'm taking a break," I said.

Cherry grinned. He said he had been watching me and

that I reminded him vaguely of a goaltender named Claude Evans. He went on to say that many authorities felt that Evans had invented the stand-up goaltending position—his theory being that since most shooters didn't really know where their shots were going, that it was best to give them the corners. Cherry said: "He just stood in the middle of the goal like a kind of tree. There was very little physical activity on this guy's part. Actually," Cherry continued, "most of his activity was down in the minors—with the Springfield Indians. He had one game for the Bruins back in the '57 season. Four goals were scored on him."

"His tactical thinking seems very solid to me," I said.

"I haven't thought of him in years," Cherry said. "Not until I saw you standing in there."

We skated slowly over and leaned up against the boards. Cherry asked what my first impressions were.

I remarked that I was surprised the practice had been so basic. "I'm even surprised there's not more conditioning."

"You looking forward to *that?*" Cherry asked sharply.

"Oh no. Just getting the goalie's gear *on* is quite enough conditioning for me."

Cherry was saying: "Of course, there are lots of theories. Punch Imlach when he had Toronto was a physical fitness fiend. He had his players up at five-thirty in the morning, running at six-thirty, and then he had these two Royal Military College instructors who gave them physical drills up on this stage in a theater—one of which was to lift up the guy next to you and hold him over your head. After all those drills Punch made the players walk four or five miles to the Arena. Everyone was so exhausted that one of the Maple Leafs goalies, coming down off the stage after trying to hold some guy over his head, fell down a set of stairs and broke his arm. I don't believe in any of that. Every bit of stuff you do off the ice, you lose momentum on the ice."

"I think your methods are just great," I said.

"We do what was done forty years ago," Cherry said.

"Are there any differences?"

"The players mostly. When I started, the college graduates made up about two percent of the players in the NHL. Now it's changed . . . up to twenty percent are college grads. The players now know how to make friends outside of hockey. Back then it was much more clannish. We had the kids off the farms, not even high school educations, and it took them a lot of time before they got worldly wise. But they were always tough, and they still are . . ."

We watched a scuffle over by the far boards between two Bruins that seemed close to the real thing, at least to me.

". . . and cruel," Cherry was saying. "If a guy's got a big nose, or if he's bald, or fat, there's no one who won't be on him like a piranha. They'll get on a guy who loses a fight . . . oh absolutely. If he gets beat up they'll call him 'Rocky' after the guy in the film who took so much punching in the face. They'll be getting on *you*. Oh yes. Wait. But it's a family. It's tightly run. Cheevers is the team leader. Very rare for a goaltender to have that responsibility. I've never had to fine a player since I've been in the league. The Chief takes them aside . . . Johnny Bucyk. I don't know what he tells them, but it works."

Bucyk himself came wheeling by. At forty-two he was not only the oldest player on the Bruins but in the entire league. He let out a whoop and yelled, "Why aren't you in there where you belong, rook', between the pipes?" the last part of his question barely audible as he sailed down towards the far end of the rink.

"It's like a big kindergarten out here, isn't it?" Cherry remarked.

I said that few sports seemed to be *enjoyed* as much by its players as hockey. I mentioned that you didn't see football

players hanging around the practice field; they trudged in
long tired lines up toward the locker room like stragglers
from a guerrilla operation. Golfers went out to the practice
tee after a round, but that was usually to fix up some quirk
in their game.

Cherry asked: "Who would want to be a golfer. You
meander along after a ball. No one hits it to you."

Bucyk came flying by again in a wind sprint against someone half his age.

The coach said, "That's why leaving hockey is so much
harder. Bucyk will be going. Very hard. It's not only the
friendships, and everything that goes with good teammates,
and all that. But the game is so much more fun to play."

Certainly that became my impression. The sport had so
many different aspects—an implement (the stick) to manip-
ulate; a projectile (the puck) to hit and pass and shoot, and
everyone got a chance to handle it—quite unlike football
where very few players actually handled the object everyone was tussling over. So much of the action of hockey was
free-wheeling, imaginative, instinctive . . . compared to
football with its precise routes and exact assignments.
Hockey had the violence too, and you could slam into
someone at twice the speed possible to generate on a football field. And then, of course, there was the particular
pleasure of hockey: that one moved across a completely
different medium—ice—that allowed great speeds, quick
stops in a spray of shavings, the ability to move backward
as fast as forward, the maneuverability of a dragonfly.

Of course, all this assumed that one was in control out
there on the ice. For me, these elements, so pleasurable to
the practiced hockey player, were foreign: the surface of the
ice had a tendency to tilt and slip, like a table top in a seance;
my goalie's stick moved with a mind of its own when a puck
approached—on occasion rising like a curtain to let it slide

underneath, or it would set itself at the perfect angle to deflect a shot into the goal. Even in moments of repose the stick seemed to be self-motivated. Once, motioned into the net during one of the post-practice sessions, I was house cleaning, sweeping the ice shavings from in front of the crease, and being very nonchalant and cool because the activity was at the other end of the rink, the stick slipped from my grasp and slid away from me. In grabbing for it, I felt my skates go out from under; and I went down on my knees with a thump, and then outstretched on my belly as I reached vainly for the stick. I pulled myself up laboriously and skated out to get it. No harm done, because the players were still at the other end, but I heard a voice from the stands call out—a teenager's by the sound of it, one of those clear nasal trumpet voices that can drift across a couple of city blocks and a park, "All *right!* Great moves out there, Bozo, great moves!"

As for the puck, it continued to be an object with which I had only the most fleeting sort of acquaintance: one would appear with the abruptness of a bee over a picnic basket, and then hum away, all so quickly that rather than corporeal it could well have been an apparition of some sort. A swarm of them would collect in the back of the net during the shooting drills without my being quite sure how they got there. Sometimes I discovered one in my catching glove, and I'd drop it out onto the ice and peer at it in surprise. And yet, in contrast the professionals seemed to have such control over a puck: in the passing drills it moved in a direct line from one stick to another, honing in with a satisfying smack to the wood. The Bruins could dance the pucks on the blades of their sticks like jugglers. They showed me how accurate they could be with them. Peter McNab, the big center, set up ten pucks at the point just inside the blue line at an angle to the nets, perhaps sixty feet away, and he wagered he could hit the far post at least three times. He did it five times—fifty percent of his shots directly on target —throwing his arms aloft at the clang of the final shot against the metal post as if he had scored a goal. I wondered what other sports could produce such examples of accuracy. Could a baseball pitcher maintain such an average against an inch-wide target from that distance—about what it was from the pitching rubber? Or a quarterback hit an inch-wide target twenty yards downfield? Certainly a tennis player would have his difficulties at that distance. A golfer would be very hard-pressed faced with a sixty-foot putt. Perhaps only the archer with his bow could compare.

They showed me how they could control a puck in the air . . . making the puck drop abruptly in mid-flight, or jump like a fast ball; they could sweep it off the ice at a tilt so that the puck came in on the net in wide curves. Later that first day Bobby Schmautz set up a number of pucks on edge and with slapshots sent them in on me in the goal like a flurry of knuckleballs, one after the other in quick succession, each darting from side to side, and in trying to block them I shivered in front of their oncoming passage like a man with the ague before they would dart and spend themselves with a slight hiss against the netting in the back of the goal.

I shouted inside my helmet. Out at center ice the Bruins grinned and called down that I hadn't seen anything yet. The most impressive shot was yet to come—the "zinger." That was the full wrist shot, the one that came in at 130 mph. The Bruins said they'd been easy on me so far, but it would be the "zinger" I would be seeing in Philadelphia when the Flyers came down against the goal. Sooner or later I was going to be involved with such a thing. Schmautz was very anxious to show me. Sometimes he smacked one against the glass off to one side so I could hear what it sounded like.

"Oh yes, you're going to have to deal with one of those,"
he said.

"You'd better keep your eye on Schmautz," I was told.
"They have a nickname for him—'Doctor Hook,' or sometimes 'The Scalper,' and that's for the way he carves people
up with his stick."

"Yes, I've heard that. Doctor Hook." I wanted to know,
"Why would he do that to me. After all, I'm on his team."

"Practice," Cheevers chimed in. "Why do you think we
have practice?"

4

USUALLY there were two practices a day—a chance between them for a light lunch and a breather in the motel room before driving back to the Wallace Rink for the afternoon session. Invariably, after practice was over for the day the local kids would be waiting at the front door of the rink for autographs. Sometimes it took the better known of the Bruins almost half an hour to break through the thickets of waving papers. The players were always very accomodating. The lesser known, those whose faces were strange, the rookies, I among them, would slope out to the parking lot, and since most of us needed rides back to the motel, or to the rendezvous at the bars, we would lean against the cars and wait.

Gerry Cheevers told me an autographing story about a fellow-Bruin of some years ago named Joe Monahan with whom he had gone with some other hockey players for a personal appearance at a boys' school outside Providence. After a short talk on hockey, the players began signing autographs. It was while doing this that Cheevers discovered that Monahan was signing the names of players who had been unable to make the trip.

"Who else do you want?" Monahan would ask a kid.

"Orr."

Monahan would write it out.

"Now who?"

"Eddie Johnston."

He'd write out Eddie Johnston's.

"Derek Sanderson . . . Johnny McKenzie . . ."

At this last name, according to Cheesie, Monahan started to write the name and then scratched his head. "Kid," he said, "you're out of luck. I can't spell that one."

I asked: "Why do you suppose these kids wanted these bogus autographs?"

Cheesie thought for a moment and then he said, "Well, I guess they reckoned that a Monahan's 'Orr' was better than no Orr at all."

After practice the majority of the players gathered in one of the taverns of Fitchburg—a particular favorite was the Peter Pan—for a number of rounds of beers. It was the best time of the training camp—certainly for me, knowing that the rigors of the day, and its embarrassments, were over, at least until the next morning.

The Bruins seemed to go out on the town as a group— quite unlike athletes in the other sports I had been associated with, who seemed to divide up and go their separate ways after practice. The Bruins would take over the back area of a bar and I would look through the late afternoon darkness to see as many as thirty of them seated around tables pulled together, the discarded beer cans, crushed, tossed in a pile in the center of the table. The conversation was lively and funny.

In fact, these late afternoon get-togethers were so entertaining that I often wondered why I had been warned that my time with hockey players away from the ice was going to be dull, certainly compared with the time I had spent, say, with professional football players. The hockey players would not have much to offer. I had been told why. They came largely from unsophisticated rural areas and in most cases jumped directly from school into the juniors and then into professional hockey, thus skipping the productive years of a college education.

The demographics were slowly changing—as Don Cherry had told me out on the ice—but it occurred to me later that this background was perhaps very much the reason one *had* such a good time with them. They had moved right from school into the adult life; they were obliged to become adults overnight. Traveling across the country, often on tours abroad for the international competitions, they became self-sufficient; they learned to entertain each other and fend for themselves in the outside world rather than going through those coddling years that a large number of athletic scholarship collegians spent sitting in the lounge of the athletic dormitory watching a morning quiz show on TV and wondering idly whether to skip the Phys. Ed. course that day. I saw many more books in the Bruins motel rooms and on the bus trips than I ever remembered from my other athletic associations. Three Bruins were reading John Toland's biography of Adolf Hitler. The backgammon game boards came out on the bus trips. A few of the older hockey generation played pinochle, or euchre. Terry O'Reilly was a chess player. Even a bridge game could be spotted. When the rookies did not know a game, their elders taught them—anything to keep minds occupied. Gump Worsley recalls a deep voice rumbling out of the back of the bus where a bridge game was going on: "Two no spades!"

But they were mainly an aural society; they soaked up the great hockey stories so they could pass them on during the long bus trips and in the taverns; it did not matter if one had heard them before: they came as a tonic and revivification.

I listened eagerly for the next Bruin to clear his throat and begin.

The player they inevitably talked about was Bobby Orr. They told stories about him with a kind of reverence, with no interruptions, or horseplay around the table, and if a waitress came around to take orders for another round of beers, she waited until the story was done, and very likely, being a Massachusetts girl, she would lean in to hear the rest of it because there was no one, ever, who matched Orr for the adulation he received in New England for his brand of play.

"He was two steps ahead of anyone," Brad Park was saying, "and then after his knee injury he was one step ahead. No one like him. Players like Gilbert Perreault and Guy Lafleur are exciting to watch . . . but they can't control a game like Orr did."

My favorite story at the tables was about Orr killing a penalty in a game against Oakland. Swinging around the ice in control of the puck, somehow in the process of some snappy maneuvering Orr lost one of his gloves at midice— it lay palm up like a huge mail fist discarded on a battlefield. He was not deterred at all. Wheeling around behind his own net, one bare hand on the stick, he came back up the ice with the puck, going at top speed, when suddenly, almost as an afterthought, he reached down and scooped his bare hand into the empty glove as he passed it, never breaking stride, and settling it into place, he went on through the two defensemen and challenged Gary Smith, the Oakland goalie. And Smith beat him, turning away Orr's shot . . . and the best part of the story was that *both* benches groaned, the Oakland bench as well, because the sequence had been so brilliant that it seemed to require a goal to round it out aesthetically.

As the waitress began to take the orders, I thumped my
hands amid the debris on the table in appreciation of what
I'd heard. Someone leaned forward through the haze of
cigarette smoke and said that when you got to talking about
Bobby Orr, it was like the winter in Buffalo—"Everybody
has a story about it."

At the end of the table the comment was made that part
of Orr's brilliance was that he was a defenseman . . . that
when he got to the puck, the expanse of ice was in front of
him to survey. He was like a quarterback dropping back
who has enough protection to select the best offensive
choice. Equivalently, Orr could spot the lanes to plan his
moves up the ice. Punch Imlach, who coached Toronto and
Buffalo during Orr's playing days, used to say that when
Orr went by the bench on one of his extraordinary rink-
length rushes he'd turn away so he didn't have to watch.

One interesting thing they told me about Bobby Orr was
that often when he scored a goal he would put his head
down almost as if in shame as he skated away from the net.
None of this running on ice and pumping his gloved hand
in the air in triumph. Orr knew that the act of scoring had
certainly embarrassed the goaltender and very likely one or
two others on the ice as well . . . and embarrassing people
was something that rather embarrassed *him.* So he eased
away, like a pickpocket, from the scene of a success.

And yet he was such a competitor that he once used his
head to block a shot when no other part of his anatomy
could be put in front of the puck. I shook my head (it was
becoming a common reaction to an Orr legend) and I said
I could hardly believe such a thing. Someone nodded and
said that it happened in the Montreal Forum—who would
forget it—and that four stitches had patched up the slice in
his forehead. The next night in a second game against the
Canadiens, he scored to break a four-four tie. He was skat-

ing almost one-eyed because his face had swollen from what had happened the night before.

They told me he never wore socks. He slid his bare feet into his skates, as if into a pair of bedroom slippers, and he never bothered lacing them up to the top.

As the evening wore on, the pile of crushed beer cans mounting up in a big pile in the center of the table (very few, if any, of the Bruins drank out of glasses) and the story telling went on, it became a very heady business for me to feel a part of the camaraderie and spirit. It was a unique sensation that I had not totally realized with other sports organizations. One would have thought that basketball teams would be the closest knit, being small in number and bonded by the exigencies of teamwork and also by the extraordinary length of the season which thrust them together, even if most of it was a slow ambulatory life in airports, it seemed, and motel lobbies. Apparently, being smaller did not necessarily make the teams more cohesive. The championship New York Knickerbocker teams of the seventies would land at the Phoenix airport and eleven taxicabs would drive off to different addresses.

Football teams were perhaps the most diversely structured. The offensive units tended to sit together in the dining halls or on team buses. Their function on the field was to execute perfect patterns, removing obstacles with blocks, all of which, if done properly, would result in the man with the ball scoring; it was all as intricately planned and put together as the interior of a watch. The defense, on the other hand, was on the field to crush this; they were destroyers, and they relished barreling about and knocking things askew. Off the field their attitudes and habits reflected this: the lockers of the defensive players were cluttered and messy, whereas the offensive people hung their sportcoats neatly on hangers. And, of course, there were

further distinctions—ethnic (the blacks tended to sit at the
same table); geographic (the Texans felt more comfortable
with each other); collegiate (the Notre Dame players were
likely to cluster together); the single Ivy League player (the
punter) sat alone by the door, and so did the side-wheeling
place kicker from Yugoslavia.

There was a certain amount of this on baseball squads as
well—the major division being between the pitching staff
and the batters. Pitchers tended to think of hitters as members of a cartel dedicated to destroying their well-being and
depriving them of their livelihoods. More often than not,
the pitchers banded together and sat in the same part of the
bus.

But a hockey team had nowhere near the diversity either
of athletic requirements or social backgrounds. There was
little difference between offensive and defensive play—the
forwards and defensive players performing exactly the same
functions. And socially, almost all hockey players come out
of small communities with names like Broken Stick, their
attitudes shaped by a rural upbringing. My favorite entry
from this kind of environment was a player named Greg
Polis, who played with the Pittsburgh Penguins, born in a
place called Dapp, Alberta, which has a population of 75.
It is wonder he ever became a professional hockey player;
often, his only competition on the ice in Dapp was a black
Labrador who came out slipping and scrabbling his elbows
on the ice as he chased after the puck.

Given so many players from this kind of background,
ethnic and racial differences were almost nonexistent. Perhaps the foreign players—the Swedes and Finns—had a
difficult time of it at the start but it was never long before
they were assimilated into the brotherhood. That was one
of the reasons for the number of fights on the ice, I always

thought; an indignity to a member of the clan was a personal affront to all.

The brotherhood was so strong and bonded that when it was disrupted—by a trade, for example—the reactions amongst the players were cataclysmic. When Phil Esposito, one of the most popular players on the Bruins in the seventies, was traded to the New York Rangers, Wayne Cashman was so upset by the front office's decision that in his hotel room in Vancouver he took the television set that was repeating the terrible news and hoisted it out of the window where it smacked onto the parking lot a number of floors below. Not fully purged of his disgust, he then telephoned room service and ordered up a hundred sandwiches—not because he was hungry in the slightest but because he wanted to stick management with the bill to indicate further his displeasure and rage. The sandwiches came on a steady succession of trays to his room. The busboys delivered them and left in a hurry. Some teammates came up. Esposito was down the hall. They tried to get him to calm Cashman down. The two talked for a while on the phone until at one point Esposito realized Cashman was no longer on the line.

"Wayne? Wayne, are you still there?"

Esposito heard a loud crash in the background. A rather frightened voice came on and said, "He's just destroyed a lamp!"

I once asked Esposito about the trade. He said it was the most devastating thing that had ever happened to him in a life which had included divorce, deaths in the family, pain. He was truly adamant about it. "It made me feel so lonely," he told me. "It was like that feeling you sometimes get in a big airport when you're moving along among thousands and thousands of people you don't know. Devastating! To walk down the corridor with my bag on my shoulder and look back and see Frosty Foristal, Bobby Orr, Schmautzie, and the others standing there watching me go. On the airplane to Oakland where the Rangers were playing, I had four, maybe five screwdrivers, and I'll tell you something: that night, playing for the Rangers against Oakland, I had one of the best games I've ever played! Two goals and two assists. I remember we lost the game 7–4. Oakland had a guy named Gary Sabourin who scored four goals from the blue line. After the game I went into the locker room and the guys were laughing and joking around. After a loss! That's when I really knew I was with a different team."

Esposito was the focal figure in one of the great Bruins legends—what they called in the Peter Pan "the great Hospital Caper." When I reached Esposito to ask him about it, he said "Oh yes! It was much better to remember that than the trade!" He said that he had been hit with a good clean bodycheck during the play-offs in April 1973, and as a result had been laid up in Massachusetts General Hospital with ligament tears ("I've got staples in there to this day"), his leg in traction, with a cast on it up to his hip . . . about as immobile as he had ever been in his life. At seven-thirty on the evening of his second day there, Bobby Orr, dressed in a white doctor's robe and a surgeon's mask, turned up in the room with a crowd of Bruins ("they'd had a few") and announced Esposito (or "Wop-po," as Orr called him, the only one who did) was going to be taken to the team's year-end wind-up party. They wheeled him out to the elevator and got him to the basement where (with Orr leading the way shouting "Emergency! Emergency!") they got him to an exit door. "There," Esposito told me, "a guy named Paddy Considine, who sits in the penalty box to keep the guys in there straight, had to rip a hand railing off the wall so they could get this gurney bed I was lying on through the front door. They ran me up Cambridge Street, lurching over the pavement; it was cold, I mean *cold*, and as we went tearing along, they kept trying to keep these blankets on me. The gurney wheels wobbled this way and that and I was scared. Orr kept shouting, 'Wop-po, don't worry about anything.' At this one street crossing, he yells at me that we're making a left turn. 'Put your hand out!' he tells me. 'We're making a left!' And you know what? So help me, I *did*. I stuck out my hand and we sailed around this corner, and eventually into this Bruins hangout called the Branding Iron. Once in there they put a Provolone cheese, which is a very strong cheese you can bet, between my legs, a beer in either hand, and Orr sings out, 'Okay, the party's started!'

"After a while the phone rings and it's Doctor Rose from the hospital. He is pissed. I mean he is really *pissed*. Livid! He tells whoever answers the phone that he's sending an ambulance. Well, the Bruins didn't want any help. They'd gotten me out of the Mass General. They were going to get me back. By this time, the front wheels on the gurney had broken, so they had to carry me. I can still see Frosty Foristal carrying the front of the bed, hurrying along Cambridge Street, the veins just popping in his neck.

"I had a livelier time in that hospital than I ever had out on the ice. One day those Italian militants came in. Crowded into the room. Tough Italian guys who showed me their guns. They were pissed about the guy who had put me in the hospital with the body check. They were all set to blow him away. They were grim, these guys. They wanted to sit up in the balcony somewhere and if they heard anybody saying anything bad about me, or even any bad reference to Italians, they were going to blow him away. Right there in the second balcony! They were very intense. Very pissed. After that, they kept the door to my hospital room locked.

"The hospital made me buy a new bed and a new door to replace what had been ripped apart to get me out through the basement. Bobby Orr said, 'Don't worry, we'll take it out of the team pot.' So after a while I got the bill —$483—and mentioned it to Orr, reminding him of the team pot, and he said, 'Well, that's interesting: we've already spent the money in the team pot.' "

It was very easy sitting in the Peter Pan listening to various versions of the Great Hospital Caper (Esposito was second only to Orr as a principal of Bruins legends) to understand what Bobby Orr meant when he once referred to the Bruins as a "team of brothers." Still I used to wonder, considering the diversity of character, how the cohesiveness they spoke of so warmly was always so solid. Were there no personality clashes? I turned and asked Rick Smith, a veteran defenseman, about controversial players such as Derek Sanderson. Rick nodded. "Certainly the two of us were different-type persons. He knew it too. After four years playing on the same team he came up to me one night after a few beers and he said, 'You don't like me, do you?'

"I went, 'Oh-oh.' I tried to explain that we were different characters. After two hours we had it straightened out. For every bad story about the Turk, as we called him, there's a good one. One afternoon after practice he took me aside and showed me some passing tricks: he made me pass the puck to him up-ice with my eyes closed. He'd say, 'I'm going to be a certain place every time.' I tried it—sort of foolish, I thought at first—but it worked: it was a valuable exercise. It helped with confidence, that sense of teamwork."

The brotherhood went by different names. It had been the Big Bad Bruins. When I was there, Don Cherry referred to his players as "the Lunch-Pail Gang." They were the best of what was meant by hard work and team effort.

He was proud of pointing out that in a hockey magazine's list of twenty-five "best" categories—best shot maker, best skater, best checker, best defenseman, best goalie, every category they could think up—there wasn't one Bruin on that list. Yet the Bruins produced one record which no one else came close to. Eleven of their players scored twenty goals or more.

Best was how the team as a unit responded to adversity. Cherry said he loved it when the Bruins got a bad press. The item usually ended up on the bulletin board. It invariably had an effect. "We're not a ship anymore," he once told me. "We're a covered-wagon train, drawn up in a circle, and they're shooting at us. I love it when we're like that."

Cheevers, the team leader, had his own, even more direct methods to put the team on the mend. Two years before in Los Angeles when the Bruins were down 1–2 in the play-offs, their best defenseman, Dallas Smith, hurt, and things looking very grim, Cheevers took the entire team to the racetrack where everyone got "ploughed"—as he put it—to the degree that the squad almost to a man was incapable of uttering a straightforward sentence when they staggered back into the locker room that evening to get ready to play.

"You should have seen them," Cheevers told me, "bouncing off the walls of the corridors."

I have always half-hoped with stories like this that the denouement would not be what one expected . . . that when asked, "And then I suppose you went out on the ice and beat Los Angeles 10–0, or something," Cheevers would say, "Are you crazy. The Bruins were blotto. They could hardly put their skates on. We went out there giggling and falling down and got beat 24–0. One guy went out and tried to skate around on his socks; he hadn't put on his skates at all."

But, of course, what did happen was that, solidified by
the camaraderie of their afternoon with Cheevers at the
track, and perhaps relaxed by the intake of beer—Cheevers
said he remembered an awful lot of belching and wheezing
along the bench—the Bruins went out on the ice and tied
the play-offs by beating Los Angeles 3–0.

Given this kind of team esprit, the veterans made a great
fuss about letting someone into their brotherhood, usually
through some sort of violent initiation, and during the training season victimizing them in a series of practical jokes. In
fact, practical jokes were a big part of the social life of the
Bruins at *all* times and—to judge from the stories—
throughout the rest of the league as well. Most of it was
simple high school locker room–level stuff—scissoring the
toes off a pair of socks, the judicious use of ice cubes in the
shower stalls, sprinkling an analgesic powder ("hot stuff" it
was called) in a player's underwear so that when he drew
them on after practice, an anguished dance would begin
there among the locker room benches as if army ants were
after him, which is indeed what it felt like.

Some of the gags were simple and harmless—aimed at
the guileless or the naive. The Philadelphia Flyers had a
player named Moose Dupont who was constantly being
told that interviews had been arranged for him with various
reporters and news service representatives; he'd get dressed
up, a tie, and all spiffy, and leave for his appointment out
in the seats—such-and-such a row in the Spectrum—and the
Flyers would peek out of the corridors on their way to the
parking lots and spot him sitting up there alone, patiently,
staring out between his knees, a solitary figure against the
vast background of empty seats.

Moose fell for this two days in a row. The third day, as
he knotted his tie in the locker room to get ready to go out

and wait once again up in the seats, he said, "Well, I'll give this guy one more shot."

The use of false teeth often turned up in the gags. Many of the players, having lost teeth in the hockey wars, wore bridgework that they would remove for practice and set in paper Dixie cups up on top of the lockers. They perched up there in rows. The most common gag was to shuffle the cups around so that after practice a player would try to settle someone else's bridgework into his mouth.

Vic Hadfield of the New York Rangers had been one of the league's big teeth switchers. A common-enough refrain in the Ranger locker room after a game was: "O.K. Vic, where are my goddamn teeth?"

One of the legends about those rows of paper cups revolved around a veteran player on the Washington Capitals. Miffed at some indignity, when the team was out on the ice, he took the false teeth out of the cups, dumped them in a paper bag to spirit them out of the locker room, and then packed them neatly (cotton around them, and so forth) in a large box and sent the whole batch to Henry Kissinger, who was at that time the Secretary of State.

On the road trips, the players were prey to any number of shenanigans. Those who were not especially "wordly" (as Cheevers put it) became involved in dreadful affronts to their own self-esteem. A famous instance was the player awakened at 3:00 A.M. by his roommate and told there was a woman waiting for him in room 302—just down the hall. Her name was Jeannine. She had seen him play earlier that night and had gone to a lot of ingenuity and trouble to get a message to him that she was anxious for a meeting. The player got up and shaved; he put on a tie, his coat, slapped on some lotion, and went down the corridor to room 302. He knocked.

After a while, the door opened. Standing in it, rubbing the sleep from his eyes, was John Ferguson, his coach.

"Yes?"

The player rose up on his toes to peer over Ferguson's shoulder into 302.

"Is Jeannine here?"

It was a question that plagued the player for the rest of his career. Even into the minors, where he eventually ended up, the mocking cry would drift from the opposing bench as he skated by: "Is Jeannine here?"

The train was the familiar form of travel in the pre-airflight days, and many of the jokes involved its use. An occasional ploy, for example, was to get a player head-lolling, eye-rolling drunk in the club car and then, when the train pulled into a station at night, to heft him out of his seat and hurry him across the platform, his shoe-tips dragging on the concrete, and derrick him into another Pullman train, settling him into a bunk, reaching in between the green curtains and disrobing him completely, shoes, stockings, underwear, and then skittering back to their own train with the clothes underarm, and his wallet as well, leaving the player alone in his bunk, unconscious, stark naked, to be carried off.

The next morning out on the rink for practice, the coach would sing out, "Where's 'Hop'?" or some such name, and the veterans would lift up their big bulky hockey gloves and smile behind them and think of "Hop" waking up with a fuzzy tongue and an awful headache in the pitch-dark gloom of an upper berth, or if he had been deposited in a lower berth, raising the window curtain to discover the train was pulling into a tank town with a name like Shepherd's Crook, Saskatchewan, Elev. 153 ft., which he could read on a water tower, and that at that very moment he was supposed to be bright and chirpy at a morning practice, yet here he was with the problem of getting back to civilization without a stitch of clothing or a penny of money.

In these days of airplane travel the moving of comatose rookies from one plane to another is too farfetched a concept, though I'm sure it has been considered. I was told that the usual practice on board planes was the mild one of removing a slumbering rookie's shoes, to enjoy watching him stalk through the airport terminal and into the team bus, stocking-footed and cursing, especially if it was Minnesota and the temperature far below zero.

Most of the players subjected to these kinds of indignities were the rookies. It started as soon as they came into the league. The traditional ritual was to be shaved from head to foot. Usually the rookie would suffer this fate in the shower, held down for the shaving, and his behind would get painted blue or green, especially if he was married, with India ink. Phil Esposito was tattooed with a small B when he was initiated by the Bruins organization.

On the Bruins the shaving was traditionally done by Frosty Foristal, also known as "The Bear" for looking like one, who would amble in wearing a white smock, a surgeon's mask, and carrying a straight razor and a jar of Epsom salts. The salts were for rubbing into the nicks that were likely to occur during the ceremony. It was a memorable experience. Foristal himself was shaved in 1968 by a five-player group headed by Ted Green, the famous Bruins enforcer of the time, who pulled him out from under the rubbing table in the trainer's room.

It was a far more stringent ritual than professional football where usually the rookies were only required to stand on the benches in the dining halls and sing their college songs. Gerry Cheevers could only remember one occasion

in his long career when the procedure was not carried out
—that was when he was playing with a farm club in Oklahoma where there were only six veterans and twelve rookies. Cheevers said, "A couple of weeks into the training
season, one of the veterans said, 'Well, how 'bout the shaving?' and the another veteran said, 'Well, why don't we
think about it this year.' "

Foristal, who went back in time (he once told me with
considerable pride) to the days when the trainers rather
than doctors stitched up the players, doubled as Boston's
chief perpetrator of pranks on other teams; he was especially innovative and busy during the Stanley Cup play-offs
—his most infamous success evidently during the St. Louis
series in 1970 when disguised as an electrician he managed
to cut the wires to the organ in the St. Louis arena. As the
two teams were lined up out on the ice for the Canadian and
U.S. national anthems, Frosty could see the organist desperately working away at the keyboard. "He was pumping his
legs, banging away and pulling at knobs. Of course, nothing
was coming down."

At this point, in the eerie silence, the Bruins broke out
with their clubhouse song:

> Ob-la-di ob-la-da life goes on bra
> La-la how the life goes on.

"Is that all there is?" I asked.

"There's more, but that's more or less the gist of it,"
Frosty explained. "It's an old Beatles song. Cheevers is the
only one who knew all the words."

Fiddling with other clubs' electrical systems was apparently Foristal's forte. On one occasion he closed down the
public-address system in the Forum in Los Angeles, forcing

the cancellation of a half hour pregame show. He proudly told me that the Philadelphia Flyers were so wary of him shorting out their amplifiers that they had a back-up system and a Kate Smith record of her inspirational singing in the days of the Broad Street Bullies just in case Frosty was able to interfere with her live performance.

"Frosty, are they going to do anything to me?" I asked.

"Don't lie down on any blankets," he warned me mysteriously.

I was quite sure that as a rookie I would be suffering some kind of indignity. In the Peter Pan as I heard about what had been done to the rookies in the past I would rear back, roar with laughter, and perhaps jot down a few notes; but sometimes my laugh would crack a bit, because I was not exactly on safe ground myself. Often I would catch a Bruin—usually Wayne Cashman, who was Master of the Revels at this sort of thing—looking at me down the length of the tavern table in a patently speculative way, perhaps the kind of look a boa constrictor casts briefly at the hamster busily and charmingly tending to its fur at the far end of the cage before the boa goes back to its snooze, knowing blissfully that the first twinge of hunger pangs will come after a while.

Eventually, I discovered what the veterans had in mind to do to the four Bruins' rookies in camp, including me, to get us prepared and helpless for the shaving and painting. "I'll bet," said Bobby Schmautz at the bar one night, "that Stan Jonathan can pick up Bill Barrett" (who was a big rightwinger), "Bob Miller, and Dwight Foster up off the floor in a blanket. Along with you."

"Me? You mean the four of us trussed up in a blanket?" He nodded.

I thought about it and said, "But that's over seven hundred pounds to lift."

Then I remembered what Frosty had warned about lying down in a blanket.

Bets suddenly started being made around the table. Pencils were worked over formulas, questions of leverage. It all seemed very serious. Wayne Cashman got on the wall-bracket phone in the Peter Pan—we could see him talking earnestly—to a "jiu-jitsu" friend of his for advice as to how he should place his money. A squabble broke out about how long the four of us had to be held off the floor. By the end of it—a good half hour of serious discussion—almost a thousand dollars had been wagered.

I suspect I was saved from being trussed up, helpless as a wild animal in a net, ready for the indignities of the initiation, by an incident out on the ice halfway through the practice the next day. In the goal I had developed a bad habit—which was that in any sort of a flurry in front of the net I would lose control or drop the big goalie's stick, which I found cumbersome anyway: I would try to defend with my hands, turning the blocking pad over to catch the puck— the sort of maneuver one might expect of someone brought up on baseball. The protective golfing glove the goaltender wears under the blocking-pad offers little protection against a puck zipping in at high speeds; eventually the inevitable happened: a puck caught the end of my little finger and sliced it open, a jagged L-shaped opening that bled nicely onto the ice; the Bruins skated up to look on with big grins.

"Hey, look here."

"Where?"

"Right here! He's bleeding."

They were delighted.

"He's bleeding on the ice."

I began to wish the wound were more impressive. Jim Kausek, the trainer, drove me to the local infirmary in his car. In the infirmary I strode through in my Bruins outfit, stockinged feet, holding my hand aloft to keep the circulation out of it. The nurses looked up curiously. Almost everyone seemed to be smiling. The doctor finished the stitching. After it was explained what I was doing with the Bruins, he said I was a looney, and belonged in a psychiatrist's office, not his. Back in the motel even Seaweed was impressed. He said, "A tooth would have been better, but at least you've made a little start."

He said that perhaps now I would not have to worry about the initiation.

No?

Seaweed explained that to bleed on behalf of the organization, especially the Union, was just about the best sacrificial gesture possible, and while I had not "given" very much, as he put it, it was probably enough to keep me from being painted, tattooed, and shaved.

"You should pay the guy who sliced you," Seaweed said.

5

D U R I N G the regular season almost all the Bruins lived in North Andover, an hour north of Boston, within ten minutes of each other, so that driving down to morning practice at the Boston Garden, their cars one behind another, was like a convoy operation.

Don Cherry, as would befit the coach, lived in the center of things. After a game in the Garden, Cherry would get back to his house, have two or three beers, take his pit terrier, Blue, for a walk, and commune with her about what had happened during the day.

Cherry had a near-symbiotic relationship with his dog. I never met Blue while I was with the Bruins but the dog was an overriding presence in camp in Fitchburg, and especially in Boston. When they saw Cherry in the morning, players would ask after him, "How's Blue, Grapes?"

"Pissed off."

The player would mumble to himself "damnation," or "tabernacle!" which was the worst thing you could say if you were French-Canadian, or whatever, because very likely if Blue was "pissed off," the practices would be tougher than usual.

Blue often turned up in Cherry's pregame oratory. He would say, "According to the Encyclopedia of Dogs, the pit terrier is the athlete of the canine race. You hear what I'm saying? Well, she was rotten and mean to me in the woods today. I thought she was going to take a piece out of me. That's the way I want you to be out there on the ice tonight against the North Stars . . . rotten, mean . . ." etc., etc.

A very high compliment was to be compared to Blue. "This new rookie Bob Miller is a bull terrier," I heard Cherry say to a reporter who looked slightly puzzled at the analogy. His pencil wandered uncertainly over his note paper. "You know what Schmautz said about Blue one time," Cherry was saying. "It's not the size of the dog in the fight that counts; it's the size of the fight in the dog."

Cherry also owned a canary named John (after John Wensink, the Bruins' enforcer), but we never heard very much about him. "Not much character," Cherry told me. "Typical canary . . . sits in the sun and peeps."

"You ever bring Blue to practice?" I asked Cherry.

"Ran right out onto the ice and began gnawing a hockey stick," Cherry said.

"What do you do after you've walked with Blue in the woods?"

"We go back to the house and have dinner together. Later on, sometimes I sit and listen to my noise machine."

"Your what?" I asked.

"The team gave it to me for Christmas," Cherry said. "It plays noise like rain, or waterfall, or surf . . . soothing sounds that can relax you. What you do is say to yourself, Well, I really feel like surf this evening. So you go and switch it on. They have two types of surf—slow and heavy. There's a sound the tape gives out which is called White Noise. Unsettling, that one. I don't play it often. I like the rain the best. Blue and I sit together and it's raining all around us."

There was never very much mention of Don Cherry's

wife, Rose. In fact, in his autobiography, *Grapes,* Blue is
mentioned far more often. Once, Wayne Cashman, com-
menting on Cherry's apparent preferences, joked to him,
"Grapes, it looks like you're going to have to get rid of her.
Too bad. I've always liked Rose."

One of Cherry's other enthusiasms was the drum that he
had played in a marching bagpipe band. "We knew ten
tunes perfectly," he told me. " 'Green Hills,' 'Marian's
Wedding' . . . beautiful, beautiful ones, but then we got a
different pipe major and he said we're going to add to the
repertoire. We're going to learn 'Black Bear' and the 'Skye
Boat Song' and some others, and the whole load was too
much. The performances fell off. We didn't enjoy it; the
people didn't enjoy it."

At the Fitchburg training camp, Cherry had neither his
drum or Blue. There was always a toast, though, to Blue
with the first beer of the evening.

The coaches tended to stay off by themselves after practice and they often had dinner at the Pickwick Arms, a few
miles outside of Fitchburg, where the light from overhead
lanternlike fixtures was muted and golden and the beer
came to the table not in cans but in thick crystallike glasses
with handles. I went with them a few times—Don Cherry
and his associates, Tom Johnson, a former Bruins coach,
and Harry Sinden, who was then the club's general manager, and also a former coach. After we'd been brought up
to date on Blue, just as at the Peter Pan with the players,
the talk inevitably swung around to legends about hockey
stars. At the Pickwick Arms the sagas went further back in
time. The one player I could never hear enough about was
the great Bruins defenseman, Eddie Shore, who played for
the team in the 1920s and was the general manager and
coach of the Springfield Indians during the 1950s. Cherry
was the resident expert on him, having played for him on

the Springfield squad. It had been a traumatic experience. Shore was a man so bellicose and eccentric that in his coaching heyday, players had it written into their contracts that they couldn't be sent to the Springfield Americans. Cherry had spent four years with him in what he called "those pits."

"He called me Mister Cherry, the Madagascar Kid," Cherry was saying one evening. "I never knew what he meant by the Madagascar Kid. I never asked him why and he wasn't the kind of man you'd ask, and he probably wouldn't tell you if you did. Nobody knew why. I hardly knew where Madagascar was. Maybe it was because he thought so little of me he wanted to send me there. As for the 'Mister,' he called everyone 'Mister.' That was the only term of respect one ever heard (if it was respect), because the rest of the time at Springfield it was all nightmare. We trained three sessions a day, two hours each. We got only half an hour off for lunch. That wasn't enough time for the goalies to get in and out of their equipment. So they'd go across the street from the arena to the lunch counter and hoist themselves up on the seats in full goaltending regalia, pads and all, and order up a hot chili. They'd gulp that down and get back across the street because you couldn't begin to guess what penalties Eddie Shore would dream up for you if you got back to the ice a minute or so late."

Cherry caught me shaking my head in disbelief. He grinned. "What a time you would have had there. He hated goalies who went down on the ice. To keep them in the habit of standing up he tied a rope around their necks that was attached to the crossbar of the cage so they couldn't go down."

"I would have hanged in the first minute," I said. "A suicide who'd picked a strange place to do it."

"It wouldn't have bothered Shore at all," Cherry said.

"He was stuck on a stand-up style. We had a goaltender named Claude Evans . . ."

"You were telling me about him the other day," I said. "I reminded you of him—the motionless, stand-up style."

Cherry laughed. "Well, he wasn't *quite* motionless, though almost. This one time, he had a shut-out going, but then he made what for Shore was a cardinal sin—he went down to block a shot. Shore fined him $50 on the spot, even though Evans had made a good save, and for the rest of the game Shore stood in the stands behind the net and every time there'd be a breakaway, he'd scream at Evans, 'Don't go down! Don't go down!'

"Shore had all kinds of crazy theories. He had an idea that you had to skate with your knees bent almost in a crouch. His image for it—which was hard to forget once you heard it—was that the proper skating position was like going to the bathroom in the woods. So his players tended to skate around like ducks. I mean literally. One day Jim Bartlett of the New York Rangers was sitting in the stands laughing at us and making remarks. Shore, skating by, noticed him, and a week later Bartlett was on the club. Shore had got him. He wasn't Jim any more. He was Mister Bartlett. He looked shell-shocked. He *was* shell-shocked. He began skating like a duck. Shore benched him for the entire finals of the Calder Cup and that was just about the end of Bartlett's hockey career."

"What did he look like?" I asked.

"Shore? Well, he walked upright, if that's what you're getting at. He looked like a cowboy. He wasn't a big man. A small cowboy. He wore the number 2 on his Bruins jersey and it looked as big on him as the numbers on a naval ship. But he had huge hands. He could grip a basketball in either palm. High balding forehead. Narrow shoulders. Never one to smile. He had lost half an ear to a hockey stick and the story was he held a mirror up to make sure the doctor was stitching it on right. Amazing athlete. He was close to seventy when I was with the Indians and he could skate faster backwards than forward. He could take the laces out of his skates and tap dance on the ice."

"What was his play like on the ice?" I asked.

"In a hockey game, he played like a car out of control in a demolition derby. But he felt there was a connection between skating and tap dancing and the ballet. He invested in the Ice Capades, you know. One year he had his players lined up tap dancing in the hotel lobby."

"And they did it?"

"Of course, they did," Cherry said derisively. "What else? He was this crazy combination of finesse and tough. Tough! You can't believe how tough he was. They said he had over 900 stitches in his body. I never tried to count them, but I don't doubt it. I know he'd fractured his hip, his back, his nose had been broken flat fourteen times, and I don't think there was a tooth in his head that was his own. Maybe that was why he could dish it out the way he did. He'd been through those wars. So we respected him. But oh my God we hated him. A tyrant! He made me wear a puck around my neck because, playing defense, I had looked down at the puck and not at the forward's chest. Cardinal sin! Oh, we hated him.

"I tell you another. He once kept me out on the ice for four hours and twenty minutes because he caught me taking a peek at the clock. All this for thirty-five hundred a year. We used to drink to forget."

"Thirty-five hundred?"

"That's all we could get out of him," Cherry said. "He was the stingiest guy you ever heard of. To keep the light bills down, we had our practices in the semidarkness. We skated around in the gloom—these shadowy figures at the

far end of the rink. You couldn't tell who was coming up
the ice with the puck. When it was payroll time, you never
knew quite what was going to happen. If the payroll was too
high for the week he'd simply fine guys for poor play which
would cut down on what he'd have to pay. He'd fine guys
for poor play though maybe the guy hadn't been on the ice
for a month!

"When he quit playing for coaching, he really ran that
barn. In this one game against the Cleveland Barons a goal
was scored which Shore did not think had gone into the
nets. So he fired the goal judge just like that—you know,
the guy that sits in the little glass cage and flicks on the red
light. He *fired* this guy. You wouldn't have thought Shore
had the right to do this, but he considered the Springfield
arena his domain; the league didn't think he had the right
either and he was fined a thousand dollars."

"Did he replace the goal judge with someone else?"

"He certainly did," Cherry said. "He put a state trooper
in there who had apparently wandered into the arena to get
out of the cold. This guy was suddenly pressed into duty.
This guy didn't object, either," Cherry said. "This policeman didn't say, 'Well, I'm supposed to be out patrolling the
street' or anything. He just stepped into that glass cage.
You did what you were told when it was Shore who was
doing the telling."

I asked: "Was he as terrifying to the referees and line
judges?"

"Oh yes. When he was playing, he'd occasionally plink
them in the rear end with the puck. Once he shot the puck
at a referee who had turned and was skating for the official's
bench to report a penalty. The guy's name was Odie Cleghorn. Shore hit him in the rear end, which from short range
was apparently rather easy to do. Cleghorn added two minutes to the penalty, and when Shore then flicked the puck

up into the crowd, which was booing him, Cleghorn decided this act was far more outrageous than being plinked in the ass, and he gave Shore a ten-minute misconduct penalty."

"Shore once got so pissed at a penalty called by the referee, a brave guy named Frank Udvari, that he pulled his whole team off the ice. The only one who did not go to the bench was Don Simmons, the goalie, who was so busy housecleaning around the net, or something, that he was not aware he had been summoned. Udvari skated over to the Indians bench and told Shore he had ten seconds to get his skaters back on the ice, or he was going to drop the puck anyway. Shore turned his back on him. At this, Udvari, good to his word, dropped the puck in the circle. It was gathered in, of course, by the opposing team.

"Poor Simmons. He looked up from his crouch and saw I guess the ultimate goaltender's nightmare—his whole team vanished and five of the opposition sailing down on him, the puck clacking easily from stick to stick as they came. Incredibly, the first four shots missed—maybe these guys were weak from laughing—and the last one caromed out from the boards at an angle where Simmons was able to leap out and smother it. At this point, with play stopped, Shore somehow got himself under control and he sent his players back out onto the ice."

"Who brought him into the league?" I asked.

"He came in from Western Canada. Regina. I'm told he really hadn't played much hockey until an older brother told him he wasn't any good. He was a teenager already. Art Ross of the Bruins signed him. Art Ross was a great figure in the history of hockey—a coach and general manager of the Bruins. What a showman he was. He'd come out on the ice with Eddie Shore, pretending to be his valet. Eddie would be dressed in a big evening cloak. The band

would play 'Hail to the Chief' or something, and Ross
would take Shore's cloak like he was unveiling him, and
carry it back to the bench. He was a great innovator as well.
He invented the hockey cage shaped like the figure three
in the back. Also the puck—standardizing its size, weight,
and density. The old pucks used to bounce around like
rubber balls.''

"What was Shore's voice like?" I asked. I could not get
enough.

"Well, he was very slow-speaking. And formal. For example, he'd refer to children as 'male (or female) offspring.'
He'd get very personal. 'When's-your-wife's-period? What-
was-period-day?' That was how he talked—a pause between
every word. 'It-was-Wednesday? Then-you-do-not-have-
relations-with-her-for-three-weeks.' He'd count on his
fingers to emphasize what he was saying. "One-two-three-
then-you-can-have-relations.' He had these strange ideas
about sex and especially sex and the athlete. Once, when the
team was going terrible, he called a meeting for all the
players and their wives, and in this little steamy locker
room, with the jock straps hanging from the pegs, he pro-
ceeded to tell the wives they were allowing their husbands
too much sex. It was affecting their play. 'Now you just cut
that stuff out!' he yelled at them.''

"He would get away with that kind of thing?"

"Oh my yes," Cherry said. "He once called in a player
named Don Johns and told him to part his hair on the other
side—thinking it might break him out of a scoring slump.
Of course, the guy did it.''

"How long did you spend with these people?" I asked
incredulously.

"Four years," he said. "Oh yes. I came out of the trenches. When I was sixteen, I was getting my heart broken.
Most of that time I spent on a kind of subsquad called the

Black Aces. Those were the players who were in disfavor. It was also called the Awkward Squad. We had to do odd jobs around the Springfield arena for Shore. Painting seats, selling popcorn, and blowing up balloons. The Ice Capades were coming into the Springfield arena. So he had the Black Aces blowing up balloons for their show. They kept them in the locker room. So many balloons were blown up we could barely squeeze our way in to dress for the game. Shore did everything in that place. He had an assistant, but all that guy ever did was open the door. Shore even changed the lightbulbs. One night he was screwing in a lightbulb, way up on a ladder, when the ladder toppled away and left him hanging onto an iron rafter with one hand like a monkey dangling from a branch. Way up there at the top of the arena."

I winced.

"Yeah. Most people in a situation like that would start yelling. But Shore looked down, very cool, past his shoulder, and asked someone far below, 'Do-you-mind-moving-the-ladder-back-where-it-was,' just as calm as if he was asking for the salt to be passed at the dinner table."

I asked: "What did the League think of him?"

"He was the law unto himself," Cherry said. "For example, between the periods at the Arena was always twenty-five to thirty minutes long. That was so the concessions, which Shore owned, could get a full workout. The League got upset about this, and they wrote Shore a letter saying the Springfield organization was going to be fined if the time between the periods wasn't shortened to regulation. So the next game, the Zamboni ice-cleaning machine went out to clear the rink between the first and second periods and broke down. Ran out of gas. Shore had seen to it. By the time he got the Zamboni fueled up and functioning, it was forty-five minutes before they could get the next period

going. The same thing happened between the second and
third periods. Shore wrote the league a letter. 'How do you
like my shortened between periods?' They gave up on him.
They weren't going to run his place. They should have
known better."

"Was there ever any relief?" I asked. "I mean, could he
be funny?"

Cherry thought for a moment. "Eddie Shore could be
funny, but not often."

I asked if he could think of any examples.

"No."

I was writing no on my pad when Cherry said, "Well, of
course, it depends on what you mean by 'funny.' One time
Shore said to me 'When I was on the ice with my hockey
stick, I used it like a scientific tool; in your hands it's a blunt
instrument.' That could be considered 'funny' if you happened to be overhearing it, I guess, but it wasn't so funny
if you were looking into Shore's face and he was yelling it
at you. No, that was not very funny. It isn't even funny
thinking back on it."

"Did you learn anything from your association with
him?" I asked.

"I never learned a thing. We used to drink to forget. The
only thing I ever learned was that if you could put up with
Eddie Shore, you could put up with anything."

I asked, "When was the last time you saw him? Has he
survived?"

"Oh, nothing's ever going to drop Eddie Shore. He's a
survivor. A millionaire. Investing in the Ice Capades. You
know, in some ways I liked him . . . the magnetism. He's
well over seventy now, but he still has the fire. Back in the
June drafts he was in the Hospitality Suite up in Toronto or
some place, and somebody bugged him. So Eddie Shore
knocked him flat."

Apparently, it was this kind of bellicosity that caused the most traumatic event in Shore's life. One night in Boston during his playing career he was rammed in a humiliating check that sent him skidding along the ice on all fours, by a Toronto player, Red Horner, blind-sided evidently, because Shore scrambled up and took off after Ace Bailey, a Toronto player who had not been responsible. Shore probably should have known it was Red Horner, who had such a thoroughly bad reputation for shenanigans of that sort that on one occasion an official scorer in Boston refused to credit him with an assist. "Give him an assist? I wouldn't give that son-of-a-bitch the time of day!"

In any case, Shore pursued Ace Bailey and decked him from the rear, flung him down like a doll, and Bailey's head hit the ice. He recovered, but he never played hockey again. He almost died. It was a very serious business. Bailey's father brought a gun to Boston and vowed to kill Shore. Shore was suspended and eventually absolved, but his reputation for being what was called an "ice thug"—what Seaweed now called a "goon"—was thereafter established. He was known as this even by people who had never seen a hockey game, and for those who went to watch the Bruins, Shore was the one certainly the most booed, and it was not good-natured either—as it is when the mayor or governor gets up to throw out the first ball at a baseball game—but intense and solemn.

Of course, that changed eventually. In one of the moving moments in hockey history, at a ceremony at the first All-Star game, which was held at the Maple Leaf Gardens in 1934, Ace Bailey came out onto the ice, moving very carefully, wearing dark glasses, to present a lineup of the all-star players with medals and sweaters. When he came to Eddie Shore, the two embraced, and down the lines the All-Stars began banging their sticks on the ice in tribute to the gesture and to the reconciliation of the two. Even so, the mood about him slowly changing, it took longer than it should have for him to get into hockey's Hall of Fame. It was finally a considerable fuss by the press and the fans—those who had held Shore in such low esteem—that did the trick.

I asked Cherry what Shore would have made of someone like me fumbling around in his Springfield empire.

"Well, you would have been a Black Ace, for sure. You would have painted some chairs and blown up some balloons."

"Yes."

Cherry paused. "I'll tell you one more interesting thing about Shore and his goalies. He made them practice in empty rinks, no one else on the ice at all, and in Springfield in that deep gloom with half the overhead lights out, they would play these imaginary games."

"Not even anyone to shoot the pucks?" I asked.

"Not even a puck," Cherry said. "Everything was imaginary. Shore would sit there in the stands and watch his goaltenders dive at imaginary pucks driven at them from nonexistent wings and making imaginary saves. These . . . what would you call them?—'surreal' practices went on for hours. One of the reasons for the formation of the Player's Association in 1966 was because of this sort of thing. It kind of drove people batty."

"What was its purpose?"

Cherry said, "Well, I think it was sort of like taking your waking dreams—the kind where you lie awake and make save after save in your imagination—and actually moving this mental exercise out onto the rink. At least, I suppose that was the idea."

"Did the goaltenders have to sweep the imaginary pucks out of the net if the imaginary forwards scored on them?"

"I don't know if he went that far."

I said I thought the exercise was just my sort of thing. "Grapes, I could make a great move out there, just a lightning kind of jab, and hold my glove up with the imaginary puck in it. I'd say, 'Hey, coach, how'd you like that one?' "

"Yeah?" Cherry smiled. "Don't forget he always had the last word. He'd tell you the puck was behind you, sitting in the netting, and if you missed another one like that, you'd be blowing up a whole bunch of balloons. The Ice Capades always seemed to be coming to town."

DON CHERRY'S defensive partner on the Springfield Indians was a player named Aldo Guidlon who had a brief stint with the New York Rangers.

I met him once. We talked about Shore. Aldo's theory was that everyone in hockey should have played for Shore for one year so that for the rest of his career he could feel the worst was behind him—sort of like going through Marine bootcamp at Parris Island.

"Did Grapes tell you about Dippy Simmons?"

"Yes, he did."

"About Hank Bassen?"

"No. Not yet."

"Well, Bassen was one of the goalies Eddie Shore tied to the nets so he wouldn't go down. Shore developed an exercise for him called 'tramping.' Bassen had to pick up his skates and 'tramp' from one side of the crease to the other, like he was a kind of chopping machine, back and forth, endlessly, at top speed. The theory was that you could train yourself by 'tramping' to get a skate in front of a low-flying puck, and not have to commit yourself to the ice with a butterfly-split, say like Glenn Hall. Bassen was like a perpetual motion machine down there in the nets. If you didn't know, and you came in the Arena to get out of the cold,

there he was down at one end of the rink—some guy with
a curious affliction, shaking from one side of the crease to
the other . . . on and on, hour after hour. It was a terrible
thing to see."

"Was there any way you could make it easy on your-
selves?"

"Well, the great trick," Aldo said, "was to ask Shore a
question. He'd blow the whistle. Everybody'd gather
around and he'd give these lengthy and very boring expla-
nations. It was a good idea to wear a couple of sweatshirts
to practice because standing listening to him you could get
cold.

"Most of the lectures were on those three basics he was
such a stickler about—that you had to pick your skates up
off the ice just so when you were skating, that your hands
had to be exactly right on the stick—a foot apart—and that
your knees had to be bent just so . . ."

"Like going to the bathroom in the woods."

"Something like that. During practice he'd blow the
whistle and call you over. He always started off by saying,
very slowly, Mister So-and-So, did-you-know-what-you-did-
wrong?"

"You'd look at him and you went over those three basics
of his. It had to be one of them, maybe a couple. So you'd
think back. 'Well, I was picking them up, at least so I
thought. My hands were OK on the stick. Knees not bent
enough, maybe.'

"So you'd say, 'No, Mister Shore. I don't know.'

" 'You-were-not-picking-up-your-skates.'

" 'Oh!' "

Aldo went on. "Once we got beaten badly—I think 11–2
—and he called us into the locker room to give us a dress-
ing-down. I thought we were really in for it—a rip-tear-
assing tirade. We all sat down, and he started off. 'The-

reason-we-lost-that-game' (and we all waited breathlessly)
'was-that-you-were-not-picking-them-up!' Imagine! Losing
a game 11-2 and *that* was the reason."

I asked, "Was there any rationale to this sort of thing?"

"Well, he was a stickler on how things should be done.
Fortunately, my style of skating was close to what he
wanted, so I didn't get bothered too much. But once, I
remember, I got involved in a break-away goal for us, very
pleased with what I had done, and he called me over ('Did-
you-know-what-you . . . etc') and he said my skates were
two inches further apart than they should have been as I
went down the ice."

"It can't be helpful"

"It's not. It makes you think too much. Hockey is instinctive. Carrying all this stuff of Shore's around was like being
weighed down with a rock. But that was his way. Everything just so. You even had to *look* right. One day he said
to me, *"There's-*what's-wrong-with-you. You're-out-of-
line."

" 'Wha?'

" 'Your-back-is-out-of-line. That-shoulder-of-yours-is-a-
half-inch-lower-than-the-other. Get-up-here-on-the-train-
ing-table. Let me-crack-your-back-for-you.' "

"And you let him?" I asked.

"Not on your life. Not me. But some of the rookies
hopped up there. What else were they going to do. He'd
work on them. *Crr-aack!* They looked terrified. They'd
flinch. 'There-you-are. Now-you're-fine.' It was a risky business being with the Springfield Indians. It's lucky someone
didn't end up being a cripple. I'm surprised Don Cherry
and I ever got out of there."

6

SOMETIMES I would leave the Fitchburg camp and get home for the weekend. That strange smell from my uniform went with me—just the faintest whiff of it, like a smokey thread that tied me to my functions up there. No one seemed bothered by it. They asked questions. "Can you see the puck?" they asked. "Have you had a fight yet?" My mother, who is eighty, saw no reason why I should go back. "Haven't you seen enough? Couldn't you talk to them on the phone from now on?"

In New York I ran into my old friend, Alex Karras, the one-time Detroit Lions defensive tackle. I told him I was playing hockey for the Boston Bruins—goaltending.

"What for?"

"Well, to get a feel of it," I said. "To write it down . . . just as I did when I joined you on the Lions."

I asked him if he had any notions about goaltending.

He looked thoughtful for a moment. "No," he said. "If you asked me if I would ever want to come back to sports," he began obliquely, "the answer is that in my next life I don't want to come back as a goaltender. No sir.

"How would you come back?"

"I want to come back as the fattest bullfighter in the

world . . . so fat that when I walk out into the bullfight arena all the people there go '*Ahhhhh!!!*'

"Too many pucks in hockey," he went on. "No, it's a fat, a very fat bullfighter that I want to be."

"What about the bulls?" I asked. It was essential to push Karras along with his fantasies.

"What bulls?" Karras asked.

"Well . . . the bulls that you—the fattest bullfighter in the world—are going to fight."

"I didn't say anything about fighting bulls," Karras said. "I said I was a fat bullfighter. I'm a fat bullfighter who doesn't sweat at all. It takes me two hours to get dressed. My people stand around watching. I have sixteen crucifixes laid out on the table. I touch them in order. I visit the chapel to pray. I go to the bullring in a mammoth Hispano-Suiza. Mammoth. Its tires go flat to the rims when I get into the car. The crowd runs along looking in. I fill up the backseat like a cork. All they see is the material of my suit of lights pressed up against the windowpanes. At the arena I walk out very slowly to where the people are waiting. The band is playing the 'Mexican Hat Dance.' I raise my arm to salute the crowd. It looks like a little twig sticking out of a great pear. They all go '*Ahhhhh!!*' Then I turn around and get ready to go back to the hotel in the square."

"Nothing comes out of the gate at all?" I asked. "No bulls?"

"Well, if a woodchuck came out, or a small pony, I could live with that. But anything else, and I'm gone, especially if it's anything earnest."

"You don't think the audience would be disappointed?"

"To see the fattest bullfighter in the world? You kidding? It's the only sport where you can look fat without being foolish. A tennis player would look foolish if he came

out, a kind of mountain in a little white outfit, with a little
racquet. People would be offended. They would tell him to
go and join a circus. But in the bullring it's all posture and
gestures. They'd cheer. They'd admire the bravery. They'd
say look, he doesn't sweat. They'd throw me a tail."

"What about being an enormously fat goaltender?" I
asked. "You might be very effective . . . just corking up the
goal mouth like a bathtub stopper."

Karras said, "I could be punctured. I understand those
pucks go very fast, maybe a hundred twenty miles per hour,
and they're hard. They'd go right through, two holes, one
in front and one in the back, and everything would be let
out, a great whoosh of air, and the fat goaltender would
suddenly give this little yell and like a balloon let loose with
its neck untied, he'd go zipping off around the ice . . . and
this fat goaltender, mammoth and content, would turn, in
a couple of seconds, into a very thin goaltender, very nerv-
ous-looking and pokey. No," concluded Karras. "The big
thing is to get through life without being punctured."

"I'll try to remember that," I said.

"Is it rough up there?" Alex suddenly asked. "Tougher
than Cranbrook?" Cranbrook was where the Detroit Lions
trained when he played.

"Oh, Lord, yes, Alex. It's got to be."

He laughed and said that was why he wanted to come
back as a fat bullfighter.

I thought afterward that it *was* probably the most physical
and demanding of the major sports . . . short of boxing. The
stories on toughness in hockey were simply legion. One I
heard in training camp involved a ten-year-old boy who
failed to check his man properly (the rules in schoolboy
hockey are just the same as in the NHL except that helmets
are mandatory) and was hung up in the locker room by his
suspenders from a clothes hook—as if his deficiencies re-

quired him to become a living effigy. The boy dangled while his fellow youngsters stared up at him in awe as they got out of their hockey clothes. At one point the team's general manager walked in and, seeing this odd sight, asked, "What the hell are you doing up there?"

"The coach put me here," the boy said.

Such is the tradition of discipline in hockey and the authority of the coach that the general manager gulped and said simply, "Well, you just stay there."

It was part of the mystique of toughness in the majors that injuries were treated, no matter how jarring or painful, as the merest of scrapes. Seaweed told me that one year when Billy Kilmer, the Washington Redskins quarterback, had his nose broken, the Redskins fans, in a symbolic gesture of sympathy, wore Band-Aids across their noses to the Sunday game in Robert F. Kennedy Stadium; that night the Bruins, skating out onto the ice to play the Capitals in Washington, all wore Band-Aids across the broad flanges of *their* noses in a show of derision that anyone would think a gesture was called for because a mere nose had been squashed.

The players were always scornful of the injuries reported on the sports pages that crippled stars from other sports, especially baseball. "Those guys don't play if they have a hangnail," I heard one of the Bruins say. Perhaps the most appropriate example of these attitudes would be Lorne Chabot's comment (he was a Rangers goaltender in the pre-mask days) that he always shaved immediately before a game "because I stitch better when my skin is smooth."

In the Fitchburg locker room, even the "lepers' room," it was easy enough to identify that hockey players were the inhabitants. The flat noses. Blue bruise marks on the pale skins. Stitch marks. Physically they all looked the same. Unlike players in other sports, who run to a variety of sizes and shapes, the hockey people more or less tend to the same conformity—short, powerful legs, large behinds—this from the skating, of course—a powerful upper torso with sloping shoulders, huge, and smooth muscled, and very rarely angular. The bodies are pale. Under the lights of the rink their faces are almost silver in the glow off the ice. It occurred to me that surely no athletes look as unhealthy as hockey players in their environment. They live their athletic lives under the mercury glow of arenas, always indoors, like plants in an atrium, and, of course, outdoors during their seasons the winter suns are wan. In the locker rooms, their naked bodies never showed the lines of demarcation that set off sun tans, however faded. I was told that at one stage of the Los Angeles Kings' history a player was fined if he showed the slightest sign of a sun tan—lolling about on a beach being just too much of a breach of the hockey ethos.

A few of the players, I noticed, had curious angry welts, like a bad case of hives—usually around the waist line, or on their backs, and particularly around the ankles. It was the skin affliction known as "NHL gunk." No one seemed to know what caused it . . . even the dermatologists who visited the teams which had incidents of it. One theory was that the gunk was caused by fiber glass particles shaved from hockey sticks and which floating around the locker room get into the players' clothing. About half of the Bruins shaved their sticks, a habit Bobbie Schmautz introduced them to, so that the locker room sounded at times like a carpenter's shop. Seaweed, who did not have gunk, told me he had allowed himself to be used as a guinea pig. Little scratches on a patch of his back were "planted" with fiber glass shavings, and other suspect substances.

"My God, did they ask you?"

"Oh, they asked me all right," he explained. "But what was I going to say?"

Some players thought it was infectious and was moved from one club to another by "carriers," like the "black spot" carried by Blind Pew in *Treasure Island.* Wayne Cashman, who had a bad case, could never forget that his welts had begun to crop up when Brad Park joined the team from the Rangers. About eight players on the Bruins were affected. I thought it had something to do with the wool outfits they wore, some reaction between the material and the sweat of their bodies, perhaps, but Frosty Foristal's diagnosis was that the rash was caused by nerves. "I've had the 'gunk' and I don't wear those sweaters," he said. He went on to mention that there wasn't so much of it around these days, and he thought that was because players didn't get as "geared up" as they once did.

Once distinctive thing about being in the hockey locker room was that one was never quite so aware of the athlete's power, so noticeable in a football environment, with three-hundred-pound defensive tackles standing around. Nonetheless the strength of the hockey player is prodigious. The first time Bobby Orr ever hit a golf ball, he hit it over the restraining wall 300 yards at the far end of a driving range. One of the warnings among professional athletes from other sports was never to arm wrestle with a hockey player. Brad Park was the champion on the Bruins. The upper-body strength was tremendous. Gordie Howe felt that the best exercise for a hockey off season was at the end of a shovel or a pitchfork. His body showed it, and there were those who felt that he could have been the heavyweight champion of the world if he had put his mind to it. Many of them, in fact, sported the flat, triangular nose of the prize fighter, though, of course, what had caved in the septum bone was the kinetic force of a puck, as smooth and hard as the hasp of an axe, rather than the comparatively pillowlike leather of the boxing glove. "If you're going to get kissed by either one of those things, you don't want it to be a puck," Seaweed told me succinctly.

The goaltenders, on the other hand, seemed a most diverse group physically. Indeed, since goaltending's earliest days there has been a running argument about the ideal conformation for a man required to stand in a goal mouth. Almost every college cartoonist takes a crack at drawing the ultimate goaltender—a circus oddity, fat and wide-hipped, lying with a schoolboy smirk in front of the goal mouth, completely blocking it, like an immense floozie or perhaps a sumo wrestler, lying on a chaise longue. When I was in college, the humor magazine published its obligatory hockey cartoon in which a vast goalie had somehow trapped the opposing team in the net behind him: their faces stared out like fish in a seine.

In truth, the earliest goalies tended to be very large, immobile sorts, whose very bulk was part of their defensive capacities. A two-hundred-pound goaltender was supposed to lend "stability and confidence" to the skaters out front. They were also short—the theory being that a goalie was better capable to follow the scurries of the puck if his eye level was close to the ice. The *beau ideal* of this goaltending type would be someone like Roy Worters, known as the Shrimp, who was only 5'3" tall. Photographs of him look as if a midget had been put in the goal mouth; standing upright it appears he could be backed up into the net, with just a nudge, packed in there. Gump Worsley was perhaps the most famous of the short, turnip-shaped goaltenders. On one occasion, hearing that Worsley had a groin pull, Glenn Hall scoffed and said that Worsley was too short to have a groin pull.

It turned out, of course, that there was no perfect physical specification for goaltending. Cesare Maniago of the Rangers came along, who was over six feet, and Tretiak of the Russians, who was as well, and then Ken Dryden of the Canadiens, 6'4" and whom Phil Esposito called a "thieving giraffe." Dryden himself was self-deprecatory when it came to his height. He wasn't sure it was an advantage. He said of himself that when he fell to the ice he was like a "derailed train."

"The rule on tall goaltenders," Seaweed told me, "is to shoot low. The idea is that they have trouble reaching down for the puck. Can you touch your toes?"

"Barely."

"Well, there you are."

"I can if I bend my knees."

"You're allowed to do that," Seaweed said with a grin. "On the other hand, the best shot on the small goaltender is to shoot high on the stick side. Of course, some goaltenders develop bad habits and the shooters get to know about them. In his early years with the Rangers Ed Giacomin used to raise his stick slightly, and sometimes they scored on him by sliding a shot along the ice."

I said, "I suspect all my habits are bad."

IF there was a common denominator among goaltenders it was that they were complicated sorts, and not easy to handle. Coaches tended not to like them. A coach's best-laid plans, perfect offensive patterns, could be cancelled in an instant by the brilliant perfidy of an opposing goaltender. And yet when the goaltenders made an error, it was blatant and obscene. The puck sits in the nets, as Seaweed once said, like a dog's mess on the carpet. Don Cherry admitted to me, "I leave my goalies alone. I don't tell them what to do. I don't know anything about it. They behave like no one else. No reverence. You know what Gump Worsley once

said about his Ranger teammates in those years when New
York was kind of struggling? He was asked what team in
the NHL gave him the most trouble. He looked at this guy
and said, 'The Rangers.' "

Cherry went on to say that goalies had to have a sense of
humor—Cheevers was one of these. He told me that one
of the famous tales about Cheevers was that in his rookie
year with the Bruins he had a bad night during which ten
goals were scored against Boston, compared to two against
the opposition. Hap Emms, who was the general manager,
charged into the locker room to complain, particularly to
Cheevers. "What the hell happened out there?"

Cheevers is supposed to have said, "Roses are red, violets are blue; they got ten, we only got two."

"Cheevers's idea is that it's only a game," Cherry said.
"He's not going to make himself sick over it. He'll just do
the best he can. If it's not good enough, the next time he'll
do better. The fact is you've got to leave your bad games
out on the ice."

Goaltenders unable to achieve this kind of laissez-faire
attitude were apt to get moody and disconsolate, especially
if they had let an easy shot trickle through. Cesare Maniago,
the dour-faced goalie who was born in a place called Trail,
British Columbia, had an easy save go by him playing for
the Minnesota North Stars, stripped off his pads and disappeared for two weeks. Some of his friends thought the
length of his absence was due to the logistical problems of
getting home to Trail where he wanted to sit down and
think things over.

One of the oft-told examples of goaltenders becoming
unhinged involved Wilf Cude, the Canadiens' one-time
goaltender. He was beaten by Dave Trottier of the intracity
Maroons—this was in the mid-1930s—and Trottier was un-
couth enough to laugh at Cude as he swept around from

behind the goal, jeering at him, and pointing at the puck lying motionless inside the cage: Cude was so incensed that he took off after Trottier, swinging his heavy stick like a lariat, obviously with the intent of bringing him down. His heavy equipment kept him from catching up; he was finally caught by his teammates and led back to his cage.

Subsequently, Cude threw a steak at his wife. He never could quite remember why—only that he had doused a lot of tomato ketchup on the steak, his napkin tucked under his chin, and was all set to fall to when his wife mentioned a harmless, inconsequential matter which somehow triggered a violent response, perhaps some goaltending indiscretion suddenly recalled such as the Trottier incident, and he reared back and threw the steak at her. It went over her shoulder and smacked up against the wall, sticking there momentarily because of all the ketchup, and then slid down. Cude decided he had been a goaltender long enough. "By the time that steak reached the floor," he once said, "I'd retired." He drove down to the Canadiens' front office and said he was quitting before they came for him "with a butterfly net."

No wonder that the goaltender is traditionally thought of as a kind of nonperson, quite apart from the other members of his team. When a coach is asked how many players he is carrying on his roster during training camp, he tends to say, "Forty-eight" or whatever, "and five goalies."

The reason for this seemed to be that the very nature of goaltending suggested that its practitioners were off their nut. My fellow Bruins averred they would not think of going "between the pipes." When I told people before leaving for Fitchburg what I was going to do, they tended to recoil, as if I'd swallowed some nitroglycerin tablets and was going to explode on them. Like Alex Karras, they would ask, "But what for? That's crazy!"

It was a difficult question to answer at the time, and no easier in Fitchburg. It was an utterly thankless position; very few goaltenders had volunteered from the start ("All right, I'll do it, just this one afternoon") but once in, like being stuck in a bramble bush, they could never extricate themselves. Glenn Hall once said, "It's the only way I can support my family. If I could do it some other way, I wouldn't be playing goal."

Gerry Cheevers became a goalie because his father asked him to. His father was a coach in St. Catharine's. The regular goalie on his son's team did not turn up for one game. Cheesie's father was too embarrassed to ask any other boy to go in there, "in the cell," as Cheesie refers to it—and so he put in his own son. The team lost 17–0. The other goalie never turned up again. As Cheesie said, "We had a pretty lousy team . . . not the sort of crowd one was anxious to show up for."

Vladislav Tretiak had become a goaltender at a tender age at the Central Army children sports school because there were not enough hockey uniforms to go around; as a come-on the coach said that anyone who volunteered to play "in the shed"—which is how the Russians refer to the nets—would get one of those available. Tretiak, who among other things hates the cold and perhaps felt he might be warmer in the accoutrements of the goaltender, put up his hand.

The coach asked, "Aren't you afraid?"

"What's there to be afraid of?" Tretiak replied. He was almost immediately hit on the head by a puck, but fought back breaking into tears for fear he would lose his uniform.

In all my research on goaltending I was only able to find one source who had truly positive feelings about playing there. Jim Craig, the Olympic goaltender who became a national hero in 1980, said that an advantage to playing goal was that you get to perform for the entire game—no nonsense about riding two thirds of it on the pines—and also—a very heady business indeed if the closet at home had only a parka and two pairs of blue jeans hanging in it—you were given all this equipment! It was like the boy in the high school who choses to play the tuba rather than the trumpet because the case is so much more impressive. Besides, as a kid you were looked at differently if you raised your hand and made the choice to play goal. No one else wanted to play goal, so the volunteer instantly acquired a certain status identified with sacrifice and self-assertiveness —the kind of awe that surrounds the soldier who in the trenches gulps and announces that he will go over the top that night and take out the pillbox with a bazooka. Glenn (Chico) Resch, once of the Islanders, reported on one occasion that all the goalies he knew were essentially shy— Glenn Hall, Jacques Plante, Tony Esposito—and taking up goaltending was a kind of compensation. "It's a chance for a shy person to be onstage," he once said.

Nonetheless, the negative aspects certainly seemed to outweigh the positive. Surely it was the most unglamorous position in sports (unless one wanted to count playing in a rugby scrum). In appearance the goaltender resembles a bottle-shaped structure, stuffed stiff as a strawman, and about as graceful. He remains so throughout the game, unlike the baseball catcher who has the chance to go up at bat on occasion, which means that he can discard the accoutrements of his trade—the chest protector and the shin guards, and so forth—and at least for a while resemble his fellow players.

And then, of course, there was the danger—the thought of trying to handle an object, as solid as a bullet head, and coming in on one at speeds up to 130 miles per hour.

It was that dimension of the job that seemed to quail even

the stoutest of hearts. I was surprised to discover that Joe
Frazier, the former heavyweight champion of the world,
once said about goaltending, "I don't want nothing coming
at me that I can't stop." He went on to warn, "Don't fool
with sports that put you on the ice, or snow, or in the air,
or in water. You won't find blacks skating, skiing, parachut-
ing, or swimming. Too dangerous, man!"

And then, of course, there was the indignity of being
scored upon—the awful evidence of the score itself; there
was perhaps nothing comparable in sports that showed off
one's disgrace so much as a hockey puck lying spent in the
nets behind the goaltender. The dropped pass in football,
the strike out . . . these were mild in comparison, as common as colds, and quickly forgotten. But the hockey goal
is different. There have been some wonderful descriptions
of what it is like for the goalie: Jacques Plante once said in
so many words, "Imagine yourself sitting in an office and
you make an error of some kind—call it an error of judg-
ment or a mistake over the phone. All of a sudden, behind
you, a bright red light goes on, the walls collapse and there
are 18,000 people shouting and jeering at you, calling you
an imbecile and an idiot and a bum and throwing things at
you, including garbage."

Gump Worsley once made a list of what had been thrown
at *him* for having let the puck into the nets: eggs, beer, soup
cans, marbles, an octopus, rotten fish, light bulbs, ink bottles, a dead turkey, a persimmon, a folding chair, and a dead
rabbit.

Certainly the most startling of the objects tossed has been
the octopus, the first of these making its appearance on the
ice during the play-offs concluding the 1951–52 season.
There was actually method in the inception of octopus
throwing: that year the Detroit Red Wings had begun to do
what no team had ever done before—streak of eight games

to win the Stanley Cup. As the streak began, it occurred to two brothers in a Detroit fish market family, Pete and Gerry Cusimano, that the perfect good luck talisman to bring the eight straight games to pass would be the octopus with its eight legs. They decided to bring one to a game. The practice was to boil the octopus first (changing its dingy gray color to a rich burgundy red) in order to make it easier to throw. "If you try to throw an octopus raw, it tends to get away from you," Pete told me. "It's slippery; hasn't got any bones or anything. If you boil it, the octopus shrivels up a bit and you can get a handle on it. Even so, you have to sling the octopus stiff-armed and kind of sideways, like tossing a hand grenade."

Weighing about two and a half pounds apiece, the octopuses were imported from Portugal, and were such a delicacy (four to four and a half dollars a pound) that the brothers' father used to moan when his sons took an octopus to the rink. "You're throwing away a meal," he would complain.

The first octopus was thrown on the ice in Detroit during the third game of the 1952 play-offs against the Canadians. Gordie Howe had just scored his first goal. Pete threw it from fifteen rows back in the promenade. When the octopus landed on the ice, George Hayes, one of the officials, went skating over to remove it. Hayes was one of the portlier linesmen around the league and Pete Cusimano remembers vividly when his hand went down to pick up whatever it was, the official's skates literally came off the ice when he jumped back; his stomach seemed to stay behind for just an instant until it too sprung back and joined the rest of him.

Seeing this extraordinary double-take-recoil, Marcel Pronovost, the big Red Wing defenseman, skated over and not knowing quite what was lying in front of him, he hit it a few whacks with his hockey stick. This made one of the tentacles move eerily on the ice which got Pronovost almost as nervous as Hayes. The players stood around in a wary circle until a groundskeeper came out with a wide-brimmed shovel and hockey's first octopus was removed.

The talisman worked. Detroit won the Stanley Cup in eight straight; octopus throwing became a tradition. "Everyone's in the act now," Pete said. "You get maybe thirty or forty octopus a year thrown out of these days. I myself have cut way back. In fact, the last octopus I threw was in 1983. It's a one hundred dollar fine if you get caught, and they can take you down to the station house and book you."

"How do the people sitting near you react?" I asked.

Pete said: "Well, what I did was bring the octopus in a brown paper bag. I always let the people sitting around know what I was going to do. Most of them took the news quite calmly. Once, though, this woman beside me let out a scream. I had leaned over and said to her very quietly, 'Look, I think you should know. I'm the octopus-thrower.' She couldn't take it."

"Have you ever thrown at octopus *at* anyone?" I asked.

"Once I tried to hit Ted Kennedy of the Toronto Maple Leafs. Missed him and hit Vic Lynn of the Red Wings. As I was saying, it's hard to throw an octopus with pinpoint accuracy."

Goaltenders, being relatively stationary, make an especially inviting target. Gump Worsley in talking about this said that perhaps the most curious thing thrown at him short of an octopus (at least the one that provoked the most speculation) was a brown paper bag which fluttered down, landed with a soft plop just off the cage, and turned out to have in it a nicely-made cheese sandwich.

Most of the time, though, the gestures from the stands are hardly as bountiful. Worsley once got hit on the temple with an egg (he with Andy Brown was the last of the face-maskless goaltenders) and was supported off the ice with a mild concussion. The police found the miscreant, a terrified high school kid, and took him down to the locker room where they told Worlsey that they would turn their backs if he had any thoughts about squaring things. Gump shook his head and dismissed the kid, always regretting it afterwards—not because he wished to exact revenge, but that he never asked to find out whether he had been conked with a hard or a soft-boiled egg.

Of course, it is one thing to be hit with an egg (or an octopus) and quite another "to face the guns"—another of Cheevers's description of a goaltender's purpose in life.

Perhaps then it was not so surprising that a common trait among goaltenders was that they tended to get ill before games. Seaweed had told me what had happened to him in his first game in the NHL. Glenn Hall, "Mr. Goalie," of the Detroit Red Wings was one of those unfortunates—the club kept a bucket for him under the bench for use during a game. Bunny Larocque of the Toronto Maple Leafs was sick so often that Frank Orr, a writer on the *Toronto Star*, was moved to sympathize that Larocque was spending a large portion of his life looking at the bottom of a toilet bowl.

As one might expect, such pressures tended to produce all kinds of rituals and procedures on the part of the goaltenders. Cesare Maniago of the New York Rangers wore a hockey sock with a hole in it. If he had a bad day in the nets, he would shift the socks around and put the lucky one on the other foot. Some of the goalies had to be ignited by some form of physical contact. The Washington Capitals' Bernie Wolfe would not step on the ice until some delegated person had come up on him from behind and whacked him solidly in the rear with the flat of a hockey stick. Gerry Cheevers always liked to have someone knock hard into him in the crease so that he could get a sense of the physical contacts to come.

Once out on the ice, around the goal itself, all sorts of measures were taken. Chico Resch was known to kiss the goal posts through the little slit-aperture in his face mask. For Gump Worsley, the attendants on home ice would paint "Good luck, Gump" in little letters just by the net post—an unsettling sentiment to discover, I would have thought, for the opposing goalie when the teams changed sides to start a new period.

There were some odd habits. Gary Smith got into the practice of removing every stitch of his goaltender's equipment between periods, all these pounds, nearly forty, laboriously removing all those different parts and then, after a few seconds of sitting there naked, starting to put them back on again. He was rather embarrassed by the habit; he excused it on the grounds that his skate boots stretched—so much that he often wore thirteen pairs of socks, one over the other, and he had to take off his equipment to make the necessary adjustments.

I once asked Don Cherry what a goaltender out on the ice, encompassed by all that equipment, did when he felt the need to go to the bathroom. Cherry grinned and said that Bobby Perreault—his friend who had lost all the pigeons—had once called "time" during a game in Providence and skated off the ice to the locker room to do just that. He took his time about it too—not surprising when you consider skinning out of all that equipment. Out on the rink, the teams kept skating around for just the longest time until Perreault finally put in an appearance and went back into the goal.

"These days," Cherry said, "they've changed the rule. Another goaltender has to come in while the first guy's off the ice. It's a good rule," Cherry said. "Bernie Parent would come out of the Philly goal to get a strap changed —or so he said to the officials—but it was really to change the rhythm of the game if he didn't like what was going out in front of him. He wanted to give his teammates a chance to puff a bit."

I got interested in the mental preparation goaltenders went through—hoping there was some mnemonic device, some trick that might get me primed for my stint in Philadelphia. My research was not especially encouraging. Chico Resch once told a *Sports Illustrated* editor that the night before a game he slept fitfully, waking up after two or three hours, starting up in bed and finding himself bolt upright staring at nothing. "It's crazy, because I never think of the game," he said, "at least not consciously. If I did, I'd become a basket case." What Resch does is to think of something as far removed from hockey as possible, like lounging on a tropical beach, and then he slips off into sleep for a couple of hours, dropping slowly down into his subconscious, where something horrible involved with hockey and being out there on the rink jars him awake once again.

Ken Dryden tried to make his mind blank before every game . . . working consciously to do so in order for his body to move intuitively to block a shot rather than consciously. At one point in his long career he kept a "book" on the opposition . . . jottings about "wrist shots, slap shots, backhands, quick release or slow, glove side or stick side, high or low, about forehand dekes, or backhand dekes, and before a game, I would memorize and rehearse all that was there." Eventually he decided, as he put it, to "trust the body and the unconscious mind."

What was odd—and must have given him pause—was that he had once tested his hand-eye reaction against his wife Lynda's on a machine in a science museum and, somewhat to his surprise, discovered that he was slightly less quick than she.

Once out on the ice, Dryden had an interesting quirk of superstition—which was that before a game started he would never glance back to watch the goal judge flipping the red light switch off and on to make sure it worked; Dryden's reasoning was that if he saw the red light that signalled a goal beforehand, it would mean a steady succession of red lights during a game.

I asked Cheevers if he had any habits or rituals on the day of a game.

"I try to be loose," he replied. "I don't go to the racetrack on the day of the game—that's my only rule. I couldn't play the Glenn Hall way—all those stories about him."

Cheevers apparently does not keep book on the opposition either. "If the shooter doesn't make the move you expect him to, then you're dead." He, like Dryden, relies far more on reflex than applied thought. "It's quicker."

I went to Seaweed.

"Do you have superstitions, Seaweed?"

"Small ones," he replied. "I would guess goalies are probably the most superstitious of athletes. I always dress my left side first. I puke. I never sign an autograph before a game. Out on the ice, in the pregame practice I always make sure to catch the last shot in my glove hand."

"Suppose you miss it?" I asked innocently.

Seaweed looked at me as if I were daft. He asked me if I had any mental exercises I was thinking of trying.

I told him I had read a great hockey writer and theorist, Lloyd Percival, who felt that a goalie should see himself as a cool gunfighter stepping out into the dust of a Texas street at high noon in a showdown against the black hat fellow.

"What do you think of that idea?" I asked Seaweed.

"He's got the speed all wrong," he said. "The gunfighter

is too slow! Those guys walk out into the Texas street like they got sticks up their pants legs. They stare at each other. One guy finally says, very slow, 'You shot my kid brother in Albuquerque,' and after a while the other guy, the black hat guy, says, 'So what?' To make it look like what hockey is, you'd have to speed the film through the projector about ten times as fast. And you'd have to have *five* black hat guys out there in the street, not one, and they're tearing around throwing this gun between them like a juggler's act in a circus. No, anything that makes you talk in a slow Texas drawl has nothing to do with hockey."

"Maybe I should talk to the goal posts," I said. "That's what Shep Messing, the goaltender of the New York Cosmos soccer club, told me he did."

"He talked to the posts?"

"I don't think he talked to them at great length, or anything. But he'd get bored with the ball down at the other end of the field. He had to talk to someone. It wasn't very weighty stuff. He'd say things like, 'Be there when I need you.' "

Seaweed said, "Well, whatever, you've got to think positive. You got to play aggressive—like an animal defending a den. You can't think of yourself as a receptacle back there in the goal."

Exactly! Someone asked me: "What's your style? Are you a wandering goalie . . . I mean do you get out of there and chase pucks?"

"No," I said. "I'm pretty much of a homebody. I tend to lounge around the hearth."

That was one of the frustrating things about goaltending —and it applies to a degree to all sports in which these unfortunates toil: hockey, soccer, lacrosse, water polo, field hockey—that the goalie has very little to do with initiating the action of a game. The hockey goaltender seems even less involved than others of the breed. After all, after a save, the lacrosse goalie can roam; the soccer goaltender serves the ball out to a teammate, often a long downfield pass that initiates an offensive rush. Or he has the pleasure of booming a long punt, or a goal kick—awesome physical efforts that often reach midfield on the fly. The hockey goaltender, on the other hand, after a nifty save almost invariably has to give up the puck to an official for a face-off. If he has time to get rid of the puck before the whistle, he does so by dribbling the puck out of his glove onto the ice by the net post for a teammate to pick up and take behind the cage, all of this done rather surreptitiously, like a spy dropping off a little packet in Gorky Park. Sometimes the goaltender has enough time to drop the puck out in front of his own stick; he himself guides the puck behind his lair and leaves it there, very neatly, to be fetched by a teammate sailing by. Small potatoes indeed!

Ken Dryden, who has written at length about the position in his book entitled *The Game,* described goaltending as being "grim, humorless . . . largely uncreative, giving little physical pleasure in return."

So, naturally, the great dream for a goaltender—along with winning a shut-out—is to somehow become involved in the offense. Goaltenders have made many assists, of course (the record to date for a season is fourteen by Grant Fuhr of the Edmonton Oilers), but in the NHL no goaltender has ever scored a goal. "The Union would go crazy," Seaweed told me. "The dead bozos would rise out of their graves."

If it were to happen, it could surely be when the opposing goaltender had been pulled. Actually, a number of goaltenders' shots with an empty net at the opposite end of the rink had come close. On one occasion Johnny Bower of the Maple Leafs retrieved a rebound, moved out with it, and seeing the open net far down the ice (the goaltender,

Gump Worsley, had been pulled) shouted at a teammate,
Allan Stanley, to get out of the way; he then let loose a
laborious shot which moved slowly down the ice; observers
watched it transfixed, only to see it miss the goal by four feet
or so. Worsley, who was watching from the bench, said later
that he would have liked to see the puck go in—after all,
as Seaweed had often said, there was a fraternal order of
goaltenders, the Union—and he shook his head and cursed
the fact that it was Bower who had the chance . . . "that
blind so-and-so!" Not long after, Worsley himself had a
similar opportunity, and he missed the net by about the
same margin—four feet—in a game against the Detroit Red
Wings.

It is unlikely that this goalie's dream will ever occur, at
least in the National Hockey League. In 1970, the official
rules committee passed an odd restriction on the goalie,
keeping him to his half of the ice—the reasoning being that
a goaltender out of the crease (where he cannot be
checked) was too susceptible to injury.

Nonetheless in Fitchburg there had been a certain
amount of joshing that finally the Philadelphia goalie was
going to have an opportunity when we played in the Spectrum. In fact, he might actually score with someone *in* the
nets!

I mumbled a bit at this. "Ahem, ahem."

We were sitting at the long table at the Peter Pan.

"Might even be a chance for a goalie to score three goals
—a hat trick!"

"Ahem. Ahem."

They talked a lot about the big Philadelphia rightwinger,
Gary Dornhoefer. "You'll be seeing a lot of him," they
said. "He'll jam you in the crease. He's not supposed to
touch you, but he likes to jam, set a screen so you can't see
what's going on out there. All you'll see will be the num-

bers of the back of his jersey—number twelve, if that's of interest to you."

"Thanks," I said.

"Oh yes, you're going to have a *tête-à-tête* with Dorny. You'll have great rapport with him."

Apparently, Dornhoefer was hugely irritating. Larry Robinson of the Canadiens had once tried to "knock the stuffing" out of him—as they put it—by checking him into the boards . . . on this one occasion with such a vengeance that play had to be stopped while workmen came out with hammers and crowbars to pry the bent-out section back into place. I asked if Dornhoefer had been cooled down by this treatment.

"No."

"None of you is going to try to help me by 'knocking the stuffing' out of Dornhoefer?"

"No."

"What happens if I get in a scuffle with him?"

"If Dornhoefer fights you in the crease, we're all skating to the bench. We'll have some water, and blow a bit, and watch. We're not fooling around with that guy. You're on your own."

I asked what the chances were of being decked by someone like Dornhoefer and shoved back into my own goal. To my relief I was told that it was a sort of unspoken rule that the goalie could not be completely brutalized. Once, in a game in the Omni against the Atlanta Flames, Cheesy chopped Willie Plett who was in the crease; Plett retaliated, so violently that he knocked Cheevers back into the net. A wild brawl ensued. The Flames players were almost as angry at Plett as the Bruins. It is just not done—taking a shot of that sort at a goalie. The referee managed to get Plett behind the glass for his own protection. They said he looked like an animal in a cage, outraged players thumping on the glass with their hockey gloves. . . . cornered in his own building.

"But don't get too complacent," they said. "These Flyers'll stand up to you. They're pissers."

T H A T evening, back in the motel room, I noticed the barbells had disappeared along with the suitcases. Seaweed's prior roommate had apparently returned to retrieve them. "Probably had a derrick with him," Seaweed said. "Boy, I can pick 'em when it comes to roommates!"

I asked what it had been like to room with Derek Sanderson.

Seaweed said that in 1972, Sanderson drove into camp in a Rolls-Royce and two thousand dollars in his pocket with a rubber band around it. "He was something back then. Everyone called him 'Turk.' He was the first guy into a big moustache. I wasn't there then but in 1978 when he tried his comeback, I was asked to room with him to keep an eye out on him. He'd been in a clinic and they were worried about his drinking. The first time after practice we went to Peter Pan's, everyone throwing five bucks down in the middle of the table for beer, and he drank down two bottles of beer while I was still trying to get the top off mine. I said 'Turk, I'm supposed to be keeping an eye on you about this.'

"He said, 'This isn't drinking. If I get into the rye, *then* I'm drinking.'

"It was sad. He had once been such a force—but now so much of it was just a gesture, holding up his finger for number one when he skated out, or making the peace sign as he went out to try a stint as a penalty killer, his skills gone really, and the money too. He would borrow a pair of socks from me to go out on the town. I'd throw them away when he gave them back; he had that skin condition, the 'NFL gunk'—big angry welts, and the Turk had a terrible case of them."

He looked at me. "I haven't had much luck with room-mates. The Turk. Wild Bill. Now you. Maybe it's a kind of jinx."

He groaned and told me what it was like in the lower echelons of hockey—the interminable rides—as long as fifteen hours—to get to Des Moines or Duluth in a the bus they called "The Iron Lung." Often when they got to their destination, the equipment in the baggage compartment was frozen. They'd set it in the shower to thaw, then put it on and go and play, skating hard so they could steam the rest of the moisture out. . . .

"Hey," he said brightly. "I have a scouting report on you from this afternoon."

"You have what?"

Two scouts, apparently, had been sitting up in the little press box of the Wallace Rink to check on the progress of various players they had recommended. Seaweed knew one of them. Before practice he asked him if the pair would write up some observations on the gawky-looking goal-tender they would see come out into the nets at some point during practice. Seaweed rattled a piece of paper from his bed. "I've got it right here."

"Well, what does the thing say?"

" 'Good size and doesn't wear glasses,' " Seaweed read. "That's a good start," he commented. "But then the scout goes on to say, 'Handles puck and stick like a blacksmith. Biggest trouble is shots on goal.' "

"Oh yes. Well, what did the other one say?" I could hardly keep my eyes open.

"The other guy doesn't say too much," Seaweed replied.

"Just one sentence: 'Has trouble if he goes down—can't get back up.'"

"Well, that's not inaccurate," I said. I looked across at him. "What's your own professional opinion?"

"You're coming along. You got to use the stick more, not the big glove, which is what guys who've played baseball do. You got to learn to keep the guys out of the crease. In your game against the Flyers you're going to have to deal with Dornhoefer shoving at you . . ."

"I've been hearing about him."

"Dornhoefer," Seaweed said. "Big Philly wing. Gary Dornhoefer. If you don't clear him out of there, you won't be able to see anything. He parks his rear right in your face. He blots out the sun. You have to chop him out of there with your stick. Crack him in the ankles."

I said, "Seaweed, I can't do that. I can hardly lift my stick off the ice with both hands. What are you talking about?" But before I could absorb his answer, I began dropping off to sleep, hoping vaguely that the mysterious Dornhoefer would not emerge through the shadows of a dream.

7

I HAD never liked the fights. Looking down from my seat when a fight broke out, I could never rid my mind of the thought that the hockey players looked like large antediluvian beetles as they struggled amongst the husks of the discarded gloves littering the ice. The famous tactic—the primary one apparently—of reaching around behind the opponent, detaching his suspenders, and pulling his jersey up over his shoulders and head so that he could not see the punches coming . . . all of this offered very little aesthetic pleasure; if successful, the victim, blind, helpless, flailing desperately, looked inhuman, rather like a damp ski sweater flopping in the wind from a clothesline. Seaweed had referred to this maneuver as "turning out the lights on a guy"—submerging him in the dark folds of his own jersey while the punches from his opponent began to dent in from the outside. Many players had special buttons to keep their shirts attached to the anchor of the hockey trousers so they could not be subjected to this gloomy fate.

Watching this from the seats, it was difficult (for me at least) to feel much more than disgust, however partisan one's feelings about the fighters. The dismay was increased by the apparent liking of many of my neighbors for what they were seeing—shouting for more mayhem . . . the mood everywhere in the arena so ugly that truly I felt I would not take my young son, Taylor, to see a professional game again.

"Dad, what are they doing?"

"They've lost their tempers. Nothing to get excited about."

He is craning to see around the big frames of the adults standing to see the action, their fists raised, pummeling the air as they shout for more. I can hardly hear my son's piping voice in the din.

The officials always let them fight too long, it seemed to me, and usually waited until the contestants were on the ice, and one of them was getting the upper hand; they suddenly leapt on the heap to pry them apart as if their consciences had instantaneously got the better of them.

"What are they fighting for?" My son's pale face looks up beseechingly. He does not seem unnecessarily horrified. After all, he plays war games in the living room; I hear the rattle of machine guns and the whistle of bullets—a sound he makes with his tongue against his teeth in some way—the thump and groans of the dying.

I say clumsily: "They are venting their rage."

"What?"

"They're letting off steam, son. One of them bumped the other too hard. They don't like each other. One of them said something to the other. Son, I truly don't know."

Sometimes it turned out even the players did not know. I remember sitting in the penalty box with Terry O'Reilly. I was not in there because of any violent outburst on my own part; it seemed an interesting place to spend a game (we were playing an exhibition against the Philadelphia Flyers in Portland, Maine) and the officials there had no objection; they said, grinning, that it was as good a place as any to watch a game from if you didn't mind the rough company from time to time.

O'Reilly had received a five-minute penalty for a brutal fight with Paul Holmgren of the Flyers, shattering the latter's lip with a big punch before the officials were able to get between them. He skated over to the box. Red-haired, he had a large Irish face that looked, in the felicitous phrase offered by a New York *Post* writer, as if it had been "kissed by the A train." As he came towards the penalty box, I could not make the comparison, because he had his head down, so that I saw the big russet mop of his hair advancing, and little else, and even once in the penalty box he kept staring down between his skates. The quick rage that had erupted out there had utterly vanished. "What did I do that for?" he asked.

"What?" I asked in surprise.

"It's an exhibition game. Doesn't really mean much. And I had to go and crack that guy's lip open. Why?"

I said, "I really don't know." It was as if I were back in Madison Square Garden trying to explain things to my son.

Afterwards, I mentioned O'Reilly's odd ambivalence about fighting to Don Cherry. The coach said, "Well, Terry's different. You never know quite what he has in mind. Maybe that's why we call him the Tasmanian Devil. Once, in practice, he skated into the cage, banged into it like it wasn't there, and when he came back to the bench he told us he was interested in what it was like to skate blind —he was sailing around the rink with his eyes closed."

I asked, "What about the fighting?"

Cherry said, "Well, he's like a Western gunfighter, a guy who walks into a bar and orders up a drink. A brash young kid saunters up and wants to take him on. O'Reilly won't

take the challenge. He won't fight anyone smaller than him.
He leans over and asks the bartender who the best
gunfighter in town is; he's the one he wants. Those are the
great fighters, the ones who look for the great fighters on
the other teams and take them on."

"Who are these people?" I asked.

"Tiger Williams, Battleship Kelly" (those names, I
thought) "Larry Robinson, Dave 'The Hammer' Schultz,
Hound Dog Kelly, Dan Maloney . . . and they're very much
alike as personalities . . . quiet off the ice, soft-spoken, and
semi-shy. I've never seen a tough guy off the ice who was
a wild man on, nor have I seen a wild man on the ice behave
the same way out on the street. It's one or the other. I guess
if you were wild both on and off the ice, they'd park you
away in a looney bin somewhere."

I remembered what I had heard "The Hammer"
Schultz's off-season hobby was—building radio-controlled
ship models, painstakingly putting them together, lac-
quered and polished, and then he would put a crowd of
miniature lead people aboard and launch them out into the
lake from the shore, sitting in his beach chair with the radio
set in his lap. It seemed such a benevolent hobby for someone who was a hockey fighter, but then his favorite trick was
to sneak one of the ship models up on an unsuspecting
swimmer lolling on his back out near the swimming float,
who would become slowly aware of the presence of something close by, and turn to discover Schultz's PT boat or the
Queen Elizabeth, or whatever, just inches away, with a crowd
of lead people staring at him from water level.

"It gave the people quite a start," I said.

Cherry smiled and said, "You'd think it would be more
like Schultz to use the *Queen Elizabeth* to check 'em into the
swimming float. 'The Hammer.' He lets you know he's

there." He said that Schultz had once pointed out that fighting was more enjoyable than scoring because scoring only took a second or so, while a good fight could be a fine drag-out affair with plenty of time to relish what was going on.

Schultz truly accepted his role. He enjoyed his title as king of the goons. It seemed to absorb him. Almost all athletes play imaginary games in their minds as a kind of mental perparation—psyching themselves up—before actually going into the ring, or out on the field, or the court, or onto the ice. By his own admission Schultz prepared for a hockey game not by imagining himself scoring goals or making long, accurate passes, but rather *fighting*—seeing himself grab some other intimidator's sweater with his left hand and flailing away with the right.

I had assumed that the enforcer was inevitably a vast figure, rather a kind of storm cloud as he vaulted the boards onto the ice; but not at all. It was really not a question of size. Schultz was not an especially prepossessing figure. Indeed, one of the famous fighters was a very small player named Dennis Polonich whose primary tactic was hair pulling, and who was indeed largely responsible for the NHL's hair-pulling rule—namely that anyone doing it gets a game misconduct penalty.

On the Bruins, when I was there, the most belligerently inclined players were Terry O'Reilly, Dave Forbes, Wayne Cashman, Bob Schmautz, and the major enforcer, John Wensink. In the lepers' room we had Don Awrey, who was nicknamed "Elbows." He sat across the way from me. A veteran around the league (he had played with New York, Montreal, and St. Louis, and he was back with the Bruins for one more try), he had a big pleasant face which belied his competitive nature. He had the record in the books for the most penalty minutes in a game—thirty-seven!—which

he collected one furious night against Montreal, meaning
that he had spent almost two thirds of the game sitting in
the penalty box.

"But why is it so important these days—the fighting?" I
asked Cherry. "Couldn't the game do without it?" I mentioned that in college hockey and European, fighting meant
a suspension for the participants.

Cherry speculated that leagues that did not allow fighting
had much more spearing and dangerous stickwork.
"You've got to allow a definite reaction. If not, you're
going to get sneaky, far more dangerous stuff. And besides,
fighting, or the threat of it, plays an important tactical part
in hockey. Intimidation," he said. "If you can make the
other guy shy away from you and back down, because he
knows you're more dominant, you've got a big advantage.
It's the same in many sports."

Cherry said where this very obviously went on was in the
corners of the rink. The players called it "mucking it up in
the corners." The function of the scrappers struggling there
was to try to control the puck, and center it out to the front
of the goal, much as their counterparts are supposed to do
in soccer. But in hockey, of course, the puck often creeps
along the curve of the boards, trapped, and has to be win-
kled out. Players speak of having a "feel" for mucking it up
in the corners. Cherry spoke of Wayne Cashman and Terry
O'Reilly especially relishing this kind of close-quarter
skirmishing, and in the closer confines of the Boston Garden a constant tactic was to shoot the puck into the corners
so that this kind of success-through-scuffling could be initiated.

Of course, Cherry wanted me to know that these players
who were good at mucking it up in the corners and getting
into the occasional fight were not necessarily "enforcers" or
"goons"; it was in the nature of many hockey players simply

to fight for the sake of fighting. Look at Al Secord! Cherry told me that once he had come into his office and there was Secord who had set up the team's film projector and was showing film clips of his best fights—to his family!

"How was the family taking it?"

"Oh, they were all sitting on the carpet cheering him on."

Even Bobby Orr, who had never had a fight before he reached the Boston Bruins, and then had quite a few, once said, "I think the odd scrap—without sticks—is part of the game."

When I asked Cherry, somewhat nervously, how often goaltenders were targets of intimidation he pointed out that a few of the more cold-blooded competitors in the league made a point of it by aiming for the goaltender's head . . . shooting for the melon. Emile Francis, the one-time Ranger goaltender, liked to tell a story about a headhunter on the St. Louis Flyers named Eric Pogue. At an early stage of one game Pogue fired high, a shot which Francis caught in his glove; Pogue called out as he skated by, "Watch it kid, I'm shootin' 'em high tonight!" Later, when Pogue happened to skate through the crease Francis whacked him across the left ankle and broke it, at which point, Francis had the crass presence to say, "Watch it, kid, I'm hitting *low* tonight."

This sort of retribution was what you were supposed to do. Backing down in a fight was against the code. I asked Cherry, "If some great bruiser came for you and you covered up, or went for the bench . . ."

"Oh, they'd drum you out of the league. You *couldn't* back down. They'd hound you out of there. You had to stand up for yourself."

I asked, "What would you do if you just weren't any good at this sort of thing?"

Cherry said, "You have to give some indication you're not backing down. This one time, some rough guy slammed Camille Henry up against the boards. Camille, who was about the smallest player in the league, was being held up there, just *jammed* in the corner, with this guy egging him on—'now, whatcha goin' to do?'—and Camille suddenly leaned forward and kissed this guy on the lips!"

I asked Cherry if *he* had a reputation as a fighter and he told me he was probably better known as a scrapper. He flailed away as best he could. He told me, "The worst feeling in the world is when your thumb gets caught in the other guy's mouth."

"Whew!"

"You do anything to win a fight. I read somewhere that Rick Barry, the basketball player, filed his nails so they became sort of a weapon. I did the same thing, just in case that ever came in handy."

"What happened in your last fight?"

"Seventeen stitches. Dennis Hextall of the Bisons. My wife said she didn't realize a fist could do such damage. I almost hit her. Blue would never have said a thing like that."

"I would suppose personal feuds grow out of this sort of thing."

"Oh, yes," Cherry said. "Milt Schmidt of the Bruins and Black Jack Stewart of Detroit. When we went to play Detroit, Milt would start mumbling half way there on the train, 'Now leave that guy, Black Jack Stewart, alone. That's my guy.' And you knew that in Detroit Black Jack Stewart was mumbling to his people, 'Now Schmidt, that's *my* guy. Leave him alone.'

"And back then," Cherry went on, "the *teams* had such rivalries. If you happened to have two teams on a train, say Montreal and Boston, if the car with the Canadiens in it was

between the dining car and the Bruins, the Bruins wouldn't
walk through the train to eat. No sir! They just wouldn't.
Wouldn't think of it. They'd go hungry rather than walk
past those guys. Why they wouldn't even talk if they happened to pass a guy from the other team on the street! Just
walk on by. In baseball you'll see Steve Garvey at first base
chatting up those guys who come down to him with a base
hit. Never in hockey. Never!"

THE standby of hockey violence was the figure Seaweed
called the "goon"—a player of limited abilities in most
departments except the ability to fight. These people were
once called "ice thugs," "enforcers" or "policemen." Boston has had its number. Among the famous names out of the
Bruins' past was Ted Green's, who went on to become an
assistant coach at Edmonton, who wears a plate in his head
from a stick fight. One night Green had three minor penalties, two majors, and two misconducts.

The function of the goon has always been very well
defined . . . to cruise the ice outfitted with the instincts and
inclination of the back-alley mugger. Very little else about
the game seemed to be of much concern. In sixty-four
games Bob "Hound Dog" Kelly of the Flyers scored only
four times though he got involved in fifteen major fights.
His comment on the discrepancy was, "They don't pay me
to score goals." In 1972, in the Canada–Russian series,
Bobby Clarke trailed the great Soviet star Valery Khar-
lamov and, convincing himself that something had to be
done about this guy who was "killing" us, he slashed the
Russian and broke an ankle to get him off the ice. Team
Canada went on to win the next three games and the series.
"It's not something I'm really proud of," Clarke said after-
wards, "but I can't say that I was ashamed to do it."

Fred Shero, his coach at the time with the Flyers, said, "If
you keep the opposition on their butts, they don't score
goals. If it's pretty skating they want, let them go to the Ice
Capades!" He had a famous policy which applied to his
teams: "Arrive at the net with the puck and in ill humor."

Sometimes a goon was sent out to entice a particular star
into a fight—to get the better man (if he retaliated, which
was for sure) off the ice for fighting. Often, when the team's
goon was sent out, the opposition countered with *its* goon.
Once, Hilliard Graves was hounding Bobby Orr and took
what the Boston bench considered a cheap shot at their
great star. Hank Nowak was quickly despatched for revenge. "Get him, Hank. Cream that son of a bitch."

Nowak went out full of determination, set to flail around,
but apparently he had not been paying attention to the
game because after a while he came sailing by the bench
calling out, "Get who? Which one's the son of a bitch?"

The epitome of the goon seemed to be Keith Magnuson
of the Chicago Black Hawks. He had two rules—don't hit
the goalie, and don't hit a guy with a wired jaw. Everything
else was O.K. After practice he would work at his fighting
—shadow boxing, feinting, and jabbing at his image in the
reflection off the glass barriers around the rink. Before a
game he imagined himself descending into a kind of jungle
mentality, in which even his stature changed—so his teammates reported—to a kind of apish posture and his voice
lowered, all aspects of his civilized behavior slackening. Just
before going out on the ice—against the Canadiens, say—
he would stand in front of the mirror and inspect the stitch
marks crisscrossing his face. He knew which was which.
"Ferguson," he'd murmur, "that's twelve I owe. Fleming,
I owe you six" . . . this sort of thing to psych himself up for
his performance out on the ice. Once out there, at the first
face-off, his defensive teammate, Dougie Jarrett, a ferocious

body-checker in his own right, would call across, "they're bringing on the Christians," and Magnuson would take a couple of last, deep anticipatory breaths. His nickname was "Man O'War"—which he loved. A teammate would skate by after a fracas and call out, "You cleaned him up, Man O'War, you cleaned him."

John Wensink, the Bruins enforcer, was rather scornful of Keith Magnuson. "I think he took lessons that it is better to receive than to give," he once told me. "The poor man. He ran into one punch after another."

Wensink was a frightening figure to look at. He had a great shag of hair and an oversized Fu Manchu mustache. He was large for a hockey player. Don Cherry said of him, "When he comes over the boards he looks like he's stepping out of the pages of Horror Comics. If he'd ever been in one of those old-time duels where you stand back to back and step off ten paces and then turn, the other guy'd faint when Wensink'd turn and flash that moustache."

Wensink had played under Cherry at Rochester, and Grapes had brought him along when he started coaching the Bruins. Wensink said of him, "Cherry est mon père."

One day we got talking about his specialty.

"How do you get started . . ." I hesitated " . . . as an enforcer?" It seemed the politest of the terms.

"I never thought of myself as a fighter," Wensink told me. "In fact, in Junior A, seventeen years old, I seemed to be the kid that everyone else was beating up on. But I was young and strong from being on the farm and throwing bales of hay off the end of a pitchfork. One day, this bully on the Cornwall Royals, which is a team in the Quebec league, was on the ice spearing our people, and running at them. The coach sent me out to take care of him. And I did what I was told. Afterwards, I felt bad, because that was *it* for him—he sort of drifted away and disappeared—but it sure opened the doors for me. Something like that happens, and the news sweeps through hockey. They'd send me out. I knew why I was being sent out. They didn't have to tell me. The score would be 5–0 against us with just a little time left and the coach'd say: 'John, go out there.' The next day the headlines in the papers wouldn't say that we got beat 5–0. They'd say, WENSINK STARTS BRAWL. Or, WENSINK CLEANS HOUSE."

"How do you start a fight?" I asked.

"It's not hard," Wensink said. "You can start them with a flick of the finger. Rub a guy's elbow. Say something."

I asked: "Is there a technique to fighting?"

"Well, you've got to be able to stand on your skates," Wensink replied. "Balance. Very important. Once you have a guy stumbling, or off balance, you've got him. A counter-punch is effective. One thing I try to do is grab the other guy's sweater up by the neck with my left hand and then hit over my left with my right. His head's got to be there no matter what he's doing to you, and if you can keep throwing your right, he's going to be receiving it where he's finally going to want to cover up."

"I should think so," I said. "What about this business of pulling a guy's jersey up over his head?"

"If you're quick enough, it can be done," Wensink said. "But you don't see it happen so much any more. After all, the first thing is to pull the other guy's helmet off. That takes time. The helmets have made it harder on the fighters. Not only is it hard to pull off, but it's very hard on the hands if you hit the other guy on the head and he's still got the helmet on."

I suddenly found myself asking: "Are all penalty boxes the same? I mean is there anything that distinguishes the one, say, in Detroit?"

"Just plain old boxes," Wensick said. "Friends joked that

pictures of nude girls had to be tacked inside on the boards to get me in there so much." He laughed. "You get to know the guys in there who keep the time. I got to know some of them pretty good."

"John," I asked. "When the time comes on the bench, are you actually told what to do?"

"You always know," he answered. "All of a sudden the coach will say, 'Take this face-off.' You know what they mean. I only had one coach who didn't treat me right in the NHL. He came up behind me on the bench and kicked me. He pointed and said, 'Every time that guy's on the ice, I want you to get him.' So I went out, but I knew the player personally and I didn't go against him. The next day I was sent back to the minors. If I'd known that, perhaps I would have behaved differently . . . but that coach . . . " His voice trailed away.

"What does Grapes say to you?" I asked.

Wensink brightened.

"He leans over the bench and he says, 'John, would you like to go for a skate now?' "

I thought to myself what a mild and yet terrifying command to unleash that frightening Fu Manchu presence over the boards. But then there were any number of paradoxes about Wensink. His favorite hobby turned out to be making doll houses. He told me that sometimes it was a tedious sort of hobby but one that gave him a lot of pleasure. "It keeps me out of trouble," he said. One of his houses was a replica of the farm house where he grew up in Maxville, Ontario —a large model that sits on the floor of his garage measuring six by four feet, just the same dimensions, it occurred to me, as a goal mouth. It has been done almost exactly to scale (a photograph of it fooled the present occupants of the farmhouse, who thought it was the real thing) with furniture inside, but no dolls, he said. "The windows don't go up and down, but there's real glass in them. Each room has lights that turn on from tiny wall switches. After a night out on the town I can't resist going to the garage to see how it looks. I try to turn on the lights in one of the rooms. The back side of the house is open. I reach in. But after a few beers my fingers can't handle it. I smash things in there, fumbling around . . . a table turns over. The next morning I have to come down with some glue."

"John," I asked suddenly. "Have you ever fought The Hammer? Schultz?"

"No, we never tangled," Wensink said. "Not yet. We look at each other. I've thought about it. I know he thinks about it too. But we never have."

"Who are the guys on that club . . . ?"

"I know what you're thinking, "Wensink said with a big grin turning up the ends of his moustache." You're thinking about the game coming up."

I nodded.

"Philadelphia has four or five of them who can go. Holmgren. Ed Van Impe who can go, and you never know what he's going to do when he does go. Hound Dog Kelly. He's a wild ball of fire. The game can be dead boring, but when Hound Dog steps on the ice, well, for sure, it's not dull any more. Dornhoefer, he can go too."

"Oh yes?"

"You'll have to worry about him. He'll be in the crease with you. He is not really an enforcer. But he likes goal-tenders. He likes them very much."

T H E consensus seemed to be that the bellicose trend that produced the era of the true goons started at Montreal with John Ferguson in the sixties, then at Boston with its Big Bad Bruins (Grapes told me that Dave Schultz of the

Flyers had once admitted to him that about a week before
playing the Bruins he had very troubled nights—"you guys
were a little nuts!") and next, Philadelphia's Broad Street
Bullies. Then almost every team got a player whose only
function was to go out and fight.

"It goes in cycles," Cherry told me. "It's changing now.
After a while, an enforcer is going to step on the ice and
he'll be gone. The officials will step in. The general feeling
will be that it isn't good for hockey. What you have to
remember, though, is that it is not only colorful—think of
the roar when an enforcer steps out there and you see his
head turning as he looks for the guy he's going to measure
—but *useful* as well: the Flyers, using their bullies, have won
two Stanley Cups.

"Actually" Cherry said, "it's not anywhere as violent as
it once was. It was twice as violent when the NHL had only
six teams. Television came in, and the fights had to be
cleaned up some. In the old days the players used their
sticks much more in the fights . . . 'Boom-Boom' Geoffrion
of the Canadiens took his stick and used it like a baseball
bat to break Ron Murphy's jaw. 'Boom-Boom' only got a
ten-day suspension for that.

"You would like Boom-Boom," Cherry went on. "He
was a rough one. He referred to himself by his nickname.
In a restaurant he'd announce, 'Boom-Boom is pleased.
Boom-Boom likes this chicken.' "

Looking into the histories of hockey games even further
back, in the twenties, I was astonished by the number of
violent fights that are described. Here is one from December 23, 1926: "Sprague Cleghorn took a stick over the eye
and later slashed back at Phillips. Cleghorn ended the game
with a badly battered eye and bruised feelings. He had
plenty to say to Montreal fandom as he left the ice." Babe

Ruth saw the Bruins play in 1927 and left the game with
the comment: "Never saw anything like it. Thank God I'm
in baseball, with its peace and quiet." Or this from a game
account in 1930 of a brawl between the Bruins and the
Philadelphia team, which was then rather ironically called
the Quakers. "Even the referee, Mickey Ion, and the lines-
man, Bill Shaver, took a couple of solid whacks on the chin
before peace was finally restored by the gallant Boston
Police, under the stern supervision of Superintendent Mi-
chael Crowley.

"It was so wild" (the account read) "that the police
suggested calling the Marines from the nearby Charleston
Naval Base . . . ." All of this happened, incidentally, on
Christmas Day in a game which the Bruins won 8–0.

As for the supposed greatest brouhaha of them all, authorities seemed to agree that this occurred on March 16,
1947, when the Rangers and the Canadiens became entan-
gled in a huge stick-swinging brawl that involved actual
fights between everyone on both teams with the exception
of Phil Watson of the Rangers and George Allen of Montreal. This in itself was odd, both being experienced and
eager brawlers, but here their belligerence was at a low
ebb, apparently, and in addition they were fascinated by the
scene before them as the two, clutching each other's shoulder pads, wheeled amongst the fighting. Watson said afterwards, "It was the best fight we ever saw."

Curiously, only three ten-minute misconduct penalties
were meted out by the officials on this occasion—perhaps
because they knew that any stricter interpretations of the
rules would have left only two people, Watson and Allen,
to proceed with the game. The evening was further noted
for Gladys Gooding's contribution. She was the organist in
Madison Square Garden at the time. She tried to bring the

people on the premises to their senses by playing the National Anthem, but the strains of the music were barely discernible through the din.

Even the coaches got into the fighting in the early days. Tommy Gorman, the coach of the Chicago Black Hawks, who was a very fancy dresser—he wore a pearl-gray hat, gray coat, and pearl-gray gloves on the bench behind the players—began whaling away at a referee named Bill Stewart who after a controversial goal scored by the Bruins made the mistake of skating over to the Chicago bench. The account I read did not specify whether Gorman took off his gloves to fight—that was *de rigueur,* of course, to discard one's gloves out on the ice—and I covet the thought of Mr. Gorman unsnapping the hooks on the cuffs of his pearl-gray gloves and skinning them off before uncorking his punches at Mr. Stewart. The upshot of all this, incidentally, was that Gorman was ordered off the ice; he left, and took his entire team with him. I see him dapper and cocky at the head of his line of Black Hawks disappearing down the players' ramp and leaving the Bruins standing out on the ice with no one to play. But Stewart showed no hesitation at all. He skated to center ice and held the puck for a face-off as if the Bruins were playing a ghostly ectoplasmic sextet of Black Hawks. The Bruins went along with it. Not surprisingly, Art Chapman won the face-off, and he, accompanied by Eddie Shore, skated down toward the empty Chicago goal, the two of them passing the puck between them until Chapman put it in. Stewart, at this point, looking toward the exit ramp for the Chicago players to re-emerge, saw that they weren't, and he forfeited the game to the Bruins. The next morning the Boston newspapers reported three different scores —1–0 (which is a forfeit game score), 3–2 (which was the score when the Black Hawks skated off the ice), and 4–2, which was the total after Chapman had flipped the puck into the open net.

Did the players who fought on the ice ever forget? Could they meet each other in the street by chance and have their antagonisms flare up again? The Rangers' Lou Fontinato was once pulverized by Gordie Howe to such a degree that in a few seconds both eyes were swollen shut and his nose was broken. Some months afterwards the two met at a banquet in Canada and were introduced. Fontinato is supposed to have said to a mutual friend, "I'm not sure I should lower my hands to shake with him." But he did, amidst smiles, so apparently these things can be forgotten.

Rick Smith confided to me that once he had hit the wrong man—Danny Grant of the Detroit Red Wings—with a wicked enough blow to send him off the ice for some stitching. Rick said, "I felt terribly guilty. I saw him after the game and apologized. I wrote him a note. I still feel guilty. Every time I see him I go up and promise him it was a mistake. He must hate to see me coming. 'Oh my God, here comes Ricky to tell me he's sorry again!' "

Rick Smith looked like the kind who would *want* to apologize—wearing a slightly worried expression on a pleasant, somewhat homely countenance set off by a flat and absolutely triangular nose. He was excellent company, being one of those rare athletes who, equipped with the aptitudes of the journalist, was truly interested in his constituency. His favorite way of starting a sentence was to say "It's interesting . . . " followed by a reflection that almost invariably *was* interesting. One afternoon at training camp Smith produced an analogy about the tough people on the Bruins. He compared them to the character actors playing professional killers in a film about the Mafia. "It's interesting," he said. "They all possess different levels of craziness. Wayne Cashman is crazy, of course. He's the guy you'd see

handling the tommy-gun, the muscles in his face jumping
as he hops out of the Buick and starts spraying the street.
Terry O'Reilly is a good, honest hood. He goes out into the
alley without a pistol and he says, 'Put up your dukes!' That
kind of guy. Bobby Schmautz is the craziest. . . .

"What sort . . . ?"

"Well, he's the guy in the film, rather nattily dressed, in
the cheap hotel room with the bad wallpaper who has his
gun in a leather case in which it sits like a dueling pistol. He
puts the case on the bed. He takes the gun out, and then
a long silencer which he screws on the barrel. He wears his
hat inside, of course, and he has this little smile most of the
time which suggests he enjoys his work. Then he goes out.
He says something when he actually does the job. 'You're
exterminated. Good-bye.'

"Schmautzie is the kind of player who scares you out on
the ice with his craziness. You don't know how he's going
to behave or what degree of craziness he's going to exert.
They have an expression in hockey that you don't want to
fool with people 'when their eyes bug out'—meaning that
you're up against something that's not quite . . ."

"The kind of guy who would be nicknamed 'Mad
Dog' . . . ?"

"Very much so."

"What about John Wensink?" I asked. "How does he fit
into your Mafia cast of characters?"

"He's really brought in from another family," Rick explained. "He played for Grapes at Rochester. He hasn't got
that Bruins background. After all, Wayne Cashman is the
soul of the Bruins—played there since 1964. The Old Bull.
Terry epitomizes what Grapes calls his Lunch-Pail Gang—
dogged, hard worker. The Young Bull. And Schmautzie is
an electric team leader—especially in the locker room
where you need that kind of influence. All of them great

hockey people—good all-around players and scorers as well
as being tough. Wensink is a specialist. An intimidator.
That's all he is required to do. He just knocks on the door
and stands there, filling it. 'The boss sent me!' "

I thought of Wensink with his wide-boned face, his bush
of hair, and his huge moustache—he often reminded me of
a very large Tatar warrior wearing a fur hat—seeing him in
my mind's eye coming over the boards out onto the ice.

"No one to tangle with at all," Rick Smith was saying.

"Do his eyes bug out?"

"Well, he once *bit* a player in a fight. It's interesting
about that because there's no more decent man in the world
than John Wensink, but he's now got that tag: he'll always
be remembered as the guy who took that bite."

"Well, I'm extremely glad all these people are on my
side," I said. "Extremely!"

I asked Rick how often goalies got involved.

"Sometimes when they least expect. Stan Jonathan from
our club was standing next to Billy Smith, the Islanders
goaltender, one night—just the two of them—and Stan suddenly uncorked a punch at him. Down went Billy Smith in
a heap. Jonathan skated away up the ice leaving him there.
No one could believe it. 'Did you see that?' "

I had always assumed that goaltenders locked in a scuffle
with *each other* would be a rare occurrence—after all they
can barely *see* each other across the vast span of ice—but on
occasion I learned they do indeed come together and like
prehistoric creatures do battle. The backup goalies, Clint
Malarchuk of Quebec and Montreal's Richard Sevigny,
fought in the two team's great playoff rumble in 1984. On
this occasion the organist played a tango.

The most all-encompassing fracas involving goaltenders
occurred in the third game of the Canadiens against Rangers play-offs in 1968. John Ferguson of Montreal got into

a brawl with Jim Neilson right near the Montreal net, and
when Brad Park, who was then, of course, with the Rangers, got involved, Gump Worsley came out of the net,
which brought Eddie Giacomin out of the Ranger net, skating the length of the ice, and Don Simmons, a goalie known
as Dippy, off the Ranger bench and Rogie Vachon from
Montreal to waltz with him . . . which meant that *four*
goaltenders were actively involved. Eddie Giacomin got a
headlock on Gump, who said, "Hey, stop choking me. I
didn't start this thing."

I suddenly recalled photographs of just such bench-clearing brawls, a blur of figures because of all the heaving and
shoving, and sure enough, amongst the players, one could
often make out the two goalies holding on to each other's
shoulders in the "waltz"; their masks stared out of the
melee like cats' faces, or ghosts' perhaps, pale, with the
haunted-eye black holes, the thin fixed slit of the mouth,
and the immobility of expression, which made their presence far more sinister than the others, whose faces wore the
more familiar contortions of rage and intimidation.

That night I asked Seaweed if a free-for-all broke out
against the Flyers next week, just by chance, if it wasn't all
right for me to stay on the bench. "After all," I said, "if all
our goalies go out, it'll probably pair off properly. I'd be
just an extra goalie wandering out there with no one to
waltz with."

Seaweed was adamant. "You got to go out. You're a
teammate. Look for someone. You'll find someone."

I demurred. I told him I was going to get into trouble
because of my inability to stop sharply. Arms outstretched,
like a lover running for his long-awaited on a railroad station platform, I would crash into my oncoming opposite
with a speed that he would obviously assume was belliger-

ent and take a whack at it. Perhaps there wouldn't be time
for me to shout at him that I was sorry.

"Well, whatever happens, don't take your mask off,"
Seaweed was saying. "And stand up."

OFTEN, when we got talking about violence in hockey,
Seaweed would swing the conversation around to New
York and the violence there. He was not alone. Others of
the Bruins were interested that I had survived living in this
city.

"You ever get mugged?"

"No. I guess it could happen."

It always struck me as odd that some of them would shake
their heads in dismay at the thought of living in such a
rough place—these men who were ignited into violence on
the rink so often, and thought so little of it.

"Oh no," Dave Forbes said. "You wouldn't catch me out
in that jungle."

One night I told Seaweed a story about John Matuszak,
the great Oakland Raiders defensive tackle. He weighed
about three hundred pounds and was as fast, they used to
say, as an enraged grizzly. After one of his best seasons he
was invited to a testimonial lunch in New York. It was the
first time he had been in the city. He had heard the rumors.
He felt the way the Bruins did. You had to look out for
yourself every minute. Sure enough, on his way walking
down Sixth Avenue from the hotel to where the luncheon
was being held, he was jostled in the midday crowd, just
slightly, but enough to know from what he had been told
that he should check to see if his wallet was still with him.
Quickly, he patted his back trouser pocket; the wallet was
gone. Matuszak wheeled around in time to see a figure

scurrying through the crowd, curiously enough—and
Matuszak remembered thinking, what a clever disguise for
a pickpocket—in a business suit. Being a great athlete (the
"grizzly's rush," and so forth) it took Matuszak about six
ferocious strides and he had caught the man just as he was
about to sprint across the avenue through the traffic swirl.

Whatever the man had done, it must have been the most
awful shock to feel those enormous hands descend on him
so quickly. What Matuszak did was to pick him up and spin
him around, lifting him to eye level, his feet a foot or so
above the pavement—and from an inch or so away he
roared at him: "Give me the wallet, you son-of-a-bitch!"

The man, pop-eyed, reached awkwardly into his suit coat
pocket, and when he had given the wallet over, Matuszak
half-threw, half-dropped him onto the pavement and strode
on, outraged, to his testimonial lunch.

The report was that his acceptance speech from the dais
upon receipt of his plaque, or whatever, was peremptory
and angry, as if he were hugely tempted to forget the award
and lace out at the audience for the horrifying behavior of
their fellow-citizens.

He calmed down eventually. He enjoyed his ice cream.
He sipped at his coffee. He walked back up Sixth Avenue,
feeling better, but wary, his eyes darting back and forth like
a linebacker's as the quarterback calls the signals.

When he got up to his hotel room, there on the top of
the bureau dresser was—guess what?— his wallet.

"That's right, Seaweed," I said. "That guy he'd picked
up was just some poor soul late for some appointment—
hurrying along Sixth Avenue, maybe even to meet his psychiatrist!"

"Christ! What did Matuszak do with the guy's wallet?"
Seaweed wanted to know.

I told him that after hearing the story I had managed to

reach Matuszak by phone—he was playing in the Pro Bowl
in Hawaii—to find out just that. He had come to the phone,
"Hello, hello," and I was describing the scenario on Sixth
Avenue, leading up to the question about what he had done
with the wallet when suddenly he interrupted me.

"Oh, that old chestnut."

"What?"

"That's one of the oldest ones in the book."

"Oh. You mean it's not true?"

I told him I was truly sorry—it was such a fine story to
visualize . . . the innocent pedestrian being hauled aloft, all
of this happening in bright sunlight (what must have the
pedestrians thought, much less the poor man himself) and
Matuszak said, "Well, I agree with you—it's a great story."

"You wouldn't mind if I attribute it to you."

After a short pause, Matuszak said, "Well, I guess not."

"That's great!"

"Just don't attribute it to anyone else."

"I promise."

"I did it—picked that guy up."

"Absolutely."

"And I sent the guy's wallet back to him."

"You did?"

"That's right. With all the money in it."

"That was very good of you," I said.

8

I T turned out Seaweed would not be going to Philadelphia. With another contingent of the team he was scheduled to play elsewhere the same night. Hershey, as I recall.

"I'm not sure I can get along without you," I said. We
were having one of our late evening talks in the dark of the
room.

"I have an idea," I said. "The thing about goaltenders is
that they are so anonymous with all that equipment on, the
mask, and everything, you could actually take my place in
Philadelphia, be truly spectacular, butterfly split and all
that, and no one would be the wiser."

"And you'd take my place in Hershey?" Seaweed said.
"No thanks."

I sighed. "Well, what's going to be the big difference
down there in Philadelphia."

"Well, you'll look out and see these different uniforms.
That doesn't sound like much—but it's startling because
you're used to looking down the rink at practice and seeing
everyone wearing the same Bruins stuff. Suddenly you'll
see these guys wearing their logos of flying pucks on their
jerseys. Their faces won't be at all familiar. You don't know
what Bobby Clarke looks like, do you."

"No."

"On the ice he's got a wide mouth with no teeth in it, just gums, and maybe an incisor, nothing else. But you probably won't see him. What you're going to see is Dornhoefer, big guy, who's going to get in the crease with you."

"You were telling me about him the other night. My sleep was fitful."

"He's like a really big, go-get-'em type dog, one of those big elk hound types, trying to get in bed with you. You've got to get him out."

"You're sure you won't let me go to Hersey?"

"No, he's all yours."

"I'll tell you about him when I get back," I said. "I'm going to miss you."

I S A T next to Rick Smith on the way down from the airport into Philadelphia. We got talking about the various hockey towns. He had a theory that the performance of the team was very much influenced by the environment in which it played.

"A team will let down in certain cities?" I asked.

"I'm not sure it's 'let down,' " Smith said, "but its play is certainly affected."

"It's interesting. I've always believed," he went on, "that there were other factors involved than the team's skill. For instance, on Long Island, when you go to play the Islanders, the visiting team stays in a place called the Island Inn, I believe, near the Nassau Coliseum, right out in the middle of nowhere; it is the most boring, depressing place . . . nothing to do, no place to go except to wander up and down these dreary motel corridors, so that by the time you're due at the rink to play, quite a lot has been drained away. Same with Washington, where the motel is out near some super-

highway, the cars roaring by, with nothing around except
a food market next door where the thing to do is to walk
up and down the aisles looking at the labels on the cans. By
contrast, there were wonderful hockey towns: Vancouver,
for instance—which was that perfect combination: an exciting city and a poor hockey team. You always came away
with two points for a win. I loved to wander through the
marinas—lot of difference between the docks of a marina
and the food aisles of a supermart! New York was a great
place to come to. I never liked it much myself, but there was
so much going on, it got your adrenalin surging: you arrived at the Garden all pumped up by the excitement of the
place. Toronto and Montreal were great hockey towns because both were in the heartland of the sport; lots of players'
families were there."

"What about Los Angeles?" I asked.

"It's interesting. All the players in the winter zones refer
to it as 'vacation time' when they're scheduled to go into
Los Angeles. It's inevitable. I remember the first time I ever
went out there as a rookie, Ace Bailey and I got so excited
thinking about visiting this place we'd heard so much about
—the beaches, the girls we imagined were just panting to
meet two single hockey players—that we took a pair of
scissors and right there in the plane we cut the legs off our
suit trousers and turned them into cut-offs. Very extrava-
gant gesture. But we wanted to be in proper California
attire. When we landed at the airport, we rented a converti-
ble and headed right for the beaches. We ran out onto the
sand. No one was there! It was then that we realized that
though the day was bright, the sun was pale; the temperature was 55, and what few people we saw were huddling
around in winter overcoats. But that's the impression whenever you go there—that you're in vacation-land. There are
palm trees. The Marriott, where the team stays, is lively,

and there's a swimming pool, and a poolside bar. You could be in Hawaii."

I remarked: "I would think the team would be affected . . . it would tend to play a less hard-nosed game."

"I think that's true," Rick admitted. He added with a grin, "But then it's a problem that also affects the L.A. teams."

"What about the fans?" I asked.

Rick said, "It's probably because I'm prejudiced, but I always thought the Boston fans were special, mostly because they adore the sport so much. They pay great attention to what's going on, and they know the subtleties. The Garden's also the best place for the great remarks. The fans seem to come equipped with these stentorian, foghorn voices. And of course what they shout is contained in the small confines of the place, so it's like having it bellowed in your ear. Many of the remarks are directed at officials. Like this: 'We got a place here in Massachusetts, Clancy, that's named after you. It's called 'Mahblehead!' I remember one that was directed at Harry Sinden, the general manager at the time. 'Sinden!' this voice boomed out. 'There's a bus leaving for Oklahoma City at eleven o'clock. Be under it!' "

"What about New York?" I asked.

"New York fans . . . well, my own opinion is that they're the crudest. 'Get a sex change and become a man!' That's a mild one. It's in New York where you hear the obscene chants."

Cheevers leaned over from his seat. He said that the New York fans were the worst for throwing things. "Sometimes you think those guys must have come out of the chimp cages at the Bronx Zoo. When they throw things, you hear this crash near the cage. You don't look. You're too scared to see what you might find lying there."

"They really go for the jugular with their personal remarks," Smith went on. "I have particular reason to know because I haven't got the prettiest face by any means. I fell over the bars of a tricycle when I was four years old, which flattened out my nose, and the pucks have been continuing the business ever since. So I really get the catcalls and the comments when I skate out there. The Chicago fans are somewhat the same but they're more lunatic, and increasingly so, ever since they began to throw the chairs on the ice, which started in the 1950s."

"What's at the opposite end of the scale?" I asked.

"The crowds in Toronto. Very high class. You see the shirts and ties there."

"And the buildings themselves?" I asked. "Do the premises have much to do with the performances?"

"Some of the places do strange things to you, psychologically," Smith said. "In Chicago, as you've probably heard, you walk up this flight of carpeted stairs to the rink. Thirty steps! I think it is. In all those years I played, every time we went to Chicago I got that same little fear after a period of play when you had to walk *down* those stairs on skates to the locker room . . . that someone behind me, probably a goaltender, would stumble and all of us, in some terrible domino effect, would topple forward into each other and end up at the bottom in a big heap.

"Chicago and those stairs were interesting because they literally, I think, had an effect on visiting teams. It was a kind of negative thing to walk up a hill to start a game . . . you reached the ice with just a slight edge off your competitiveness. In Minnesota, come to think of it, the players come down a set of stairs onto the rink. You soar out onto the ice.

"In the new buildings they've built out in the west the crowds seemed removed and quiet. It may have something to do with the physical structure of the building itself: it sucks up the sound so that sometimes playing in one of them is as quiet as practice in an empty rink . . . the puck hitting the sticks with a crack that reverberates all over the place.

"Some of the arenas, notably the one in Buffalo, are not air-conditioned. So that when the heat of a hot spring day during play-off time, say, flows down on the ice, it can produce a fog cloud. In 1975 during the Flyers–Sabres playoff the fog was so thick that the goaltenders couldn't pick up the puck until it was well within the blue line. Bernie Parent, the goaltender for the Philadelphia Flyers, said an interesting thing about that particular game—that if there were no players at his end the fog would begin to thicken. It was only when the puck came down to him that the fog would be thinned out by the players swirling through it. 'So I was penalized,' he said, 'when the puck was down at the other goal. The fog would get so thick that I could move it with my stick. I played with it . . . like it was a toy.' "

"Wasn't it in Buffalo where Jim Lorentz killed the bat?" someone asked.

"That's right." Another of the Bruins knew all about it. He leaned across the seats to tell us. "The Flyers were in there. The bat showed up about ten minutes into the first period. Parent took a swing at it with his goalie's stick and missed and it went up ice and got into the middle of a face-off. Lorentz was upset anyway because the Sabres were down 2–0 and maybe he didn't like bats. Anyway, he took a swipe and that was it for the bat. It fell in front of Rick MacLeish. No one else wanted anything to do with it. Rick took it over to the penalty box—in his bare hand, what's more."

"What was the reaction?" I asked.

"I know Jim got a lot of negative mail. 'Poor defenseless creature' . . . that sort of stuff. A naturalist wanted to take

him to court and thought he ought to be jailed. A policeman
sent him a silver bullet. Jim wished it never happened, I
know that. He told me the bat didn't flutter; it came in a
straight line—suicidal, he thought. He loves animals. He
does a lot of trout fishing—and says he releases every fish
he catches."

"How do you suppose the bat got in there?" I asked.

"Jim always had an idea a fan had brought it in in a paper
bag. When you get to know something about fans, it
wouldn't be all that surprising."

I turned back to Rick Smith. The bus was coming up the
ramp to the Spectrum. The nerves were beginning to flutter
in my stomach. The bus was quiet.

"What about Philadelphia?" I asked.

Rick smiled and said he knew I'd get around to asking
that before long. "It's a hockey town that's good to get out
of," he said. "They may not carry bats in paper bags, but
the teams are tough and so are the fans. It was in Philadelphia that the Boston players began to get into scraps not
only with the opposition but with the crowd in the seats.
Derek Sanderson, Cashman, Ace Bailey—all of them went
over the glass to get into the stands, and the glass barriers
are high. I don't think I could get over one if you gave me
a leg up. Lots of altercations. The home of the Broad Street
Bullies. It's in Philadelphia that they first set up portable
canopies over the runway to keep the players from being
pelted as they skated out onto the ice. Rough place. There's
always that kind of twinge of fear when you're going in
there: you're moving into a danger zone."

"I'm sorry I asked," I said. "I should have insisted on
Vancouver for my stint. Or Los Angeles."

"Vancouver," Rick said. "Before the game we could
have walked down through the marinas."

9

M Y game jersey was handed to me. It had a big pair of zeroes on it like the spectacles on the back of a cobra's head. Two zeroes. With the Detroit Lions I had worn a single zero, which they joked was an indication of my talent. Presumably, the Bruins had the same sort of thing in mind, compounding it with an extra zero. When I skinned it on, I was fully dressed, goalie's pads strapped on and all. It was almost an hour before we were due on the ice. It seemed as good a way to pass the time as any. The rest of the Bruins sat around in the Spectrum's visitors' locker room in the first layer of their hockey apparel—the long white union suits—and played cards, or chatted easily . . . distanced increasingly from me now by their nonchalant calm. From time to time a player took a skate into an adjoining room to have its edges sharpened. A slight hum rose. Each hockey team carries its own skate-sharpening machine with it—a small electric lathe with a steel attachment for holding the skate in place. The equipment manager is responsible for the device and he strains his way through the airline terminals hauling the big tin-surfaced suitcases with the assembly within—the overall weight well over eighty pounds. Years ago the home team provided skate-sharpening facilities for the visitors, but it was feared that home-team chauvinism

would ultimately prevail and that the machine would be
tampered with—the edges of the skates dulled rather than
sharpened, so that a player would rush onto the ice at a
crucial moment to discover he was skating on what felt like
a pair of spoons. A few years ago the Pittsburgh Penguins
had their skate-sharpening suitcase stolen—presumably by
a thief first threatened by the weight of his booty as he tried
to scamper away with it, and then excited by the prospect
of its contents—"What could be in this thing . . . so damn
heavy . . . full of watches perhaps"—and then his ultimate
bewilderment at wedging open the tin lid to discover what
must surely be one of the more specialized machines around
—a skate sharpener.

Don Cherry sat down next to me. He saw me fully
dressed and said, "Well, at least I've got one man ready to
send out."

I smiled at him weakly. He went on to say how amazing
it was that nothing was consistent about how professionals
prepared for a game. "Bobby Orr was the earliest I ever
saw in the locker room," he said. "If it was an eight o'clock
game, he'd get there at three in the afternoon. He'd pace
around with a big weighted stick like he had nothing in his
hands. He'd get half-dressed. He'd tape and retape his
sticks until game time. Then you have the guys who come
in late. Wayne Cashman comes in late. Brad Park comes in
ten minutes before the team's due on the ice for the warm-
ups. It doesn't seem to make any difference." Cherry
paused and tapped my goalie's pads. "But I don't know any
players who get completely dressed so early before a game.
When are you going to put on your face mask?"

"Very soon," I said.

He began telling me about some of the pregame rituals.
Phil Esposito laid out his sticks in a certain way, and his
gloves too, and if anyone rearranged them, or stepped on

a stick, there was always a big commotion. Just before going
out on the ice Bobby Orr always went around the locker
room and touched everyone with his stick and Terry
O'Reilly carried on the ritual with the current team.

"Do you have any rituals?" Cherry asked.

"A lot of sweating," I said.

"I can see."

A few nights before, during one of our lengthy talk
sessions, Seaweed had described a curious pregame ritual—
the behavior of a fellow goaltender named David Reese
with whom he played on the Bruins' farm club at Rochester.
"Dave and I were sitting on our stools talking before a
game," Seaweed had told me, "discussing the players on
the other team . . . just a normal sort of conversation except
that I noticed Reese kept looking up at the clock on the
locker room wall like he had an appointment. Suddenly he
quit talking in the middle of a sentence. He had just said,
"Now you've got to watch this guy because he comes down
the ice and cuts . . .' and that was the end of it, like he'd
been gagged. And from that time on he never spoke a
word. That was his ritual—that exactly an hour before play
he'd quit talking."

"That's the damnedest thing."

"That's why he kept peeking a look at the clock," Seaweed said. "So's to know when to clam up. He made it hard
on himself, because if he wanted something real bad, or had
something real important on his mind to say, he wouldn't
allow himself to break that ritual. If he wanted something
to drink he'd point down his throat with his fingers, or if
it was something else, he'd wave his hands around and look
at you with this pleading look, hoping you'd understand
what he wanted. But he never said anything, ever. In fact,
he never said a word until after a game was over . . . just
a lot of nodding and finger waving."

I told Don Cherry about Reese and he nodded and said it didn't surprise him a bit. Tension could make hockey players do amazing things. He told me about the 1975 play-offs, when the New York Islanders carried around a fifty-pound sack of elephant dung to bring them luck. It had mysteriously arrived special delivery when the club was three games down to the Pittsburgh Penguins. It came with no return address in a big potato sack. Nobody knew who had sent it, or the significance of it being sent. Obviously, it could have been an indication of someone's extreme displeasure. On the other hand, the Islanders had been successful in Madison Square Garden in the first play-off series against the Rangers. The Ringling Brothers Circus was in town; a strong circus smell was in the locker room; somebody may have made the connection. So they took the sack to Pittsburgh and it worked. By then a talisman of high value, it disappeared just before their final play-off game with the Philadelphia Flyers. As Cherry told this, I could not help imagining the same thief who had snitched the skate-sharpening suitcase from the Penguins also snatching up the elephant dung from the Islanders' locker room ("Boy! A double heist") and his reaction after opening first one, then the other, in a back alley somewhere.

S I T T I N G in the Spectrum locker room, it was oddly intimidating, a foreign place—stools, the wire mesh of the lockers, the colors . . . all were jarring. The players said you could always tell by looking at a visiting locker room whether the team occupying it was winning or losing. The losing clubs tended to creep into a locker room and leave it in the same condition they found it, almost as if they didn't wish to leave the slightest evidence of their presence. A locker room attendant in Madison Square Garden described to me a Washington goaltender in the early, dismaying days of that franchise carefully arranging a towel at his feet in the locker room before hawking and spitting into it. The Capital players sucked oranges and lobbed the rinds toward a big plastic barrel in the middle of the room with dead-center accuracy—the oranges arcing and dropping in like perfectly executed foul shots in basketball . . . almost as if to prove that this was one physical act they could pull off without humiliation.

That was not the way, apparently, with the great dynastic powers—the Montreal Canadiens, the Bruins, the Islanders, the Oilers, and so forth. As soon as they walked in, the place began to go to pieces. Their people sucked the oranges dry and simply dropped them on the floor. Then they stood up and stomped over them with their skates and ground the rinds into the carpet; the towels were strewn everywhere. They did not set a towel down like the Capital goalie. They went ahead and spit.

The attendant who told me this said he had always looked forward to the Capitals coming to town. "It's a pleasure working for these guys," he said. "But I wouldn't want to bet on them."

W E went out on the ice for the warm-ups—fifteen minutes. The Flyers populated a half of the ice. It was true what Seaweed had observed—that the sight of them in the white and orange of their jerseys was an intrusion—like the strangeness of the Spectrum locker room—on one's sense of well-being . . . as if a gang of complete strangers had suddenly materialized in one's house. My tendency was to sneak awed looks at them. Which one was Dornhoefer? There was not much time to speculate because the pregame drills were hectic—a lot of activity all very carefully programmed to the minute. Skating drills to get the muscles loose. Shooting drills. The goalies took their turns. The arena was filling—a low hum starting to rise as the moments passed. A buzzer went off. Our time was done.

"How was the warm-up?" Cheevers asked in the locker room.

I replied. "Tense, I felt tense, and afterwards there were enough pucks in the back of the net to remove with a shovel."

"Don't worry about it," he said. "I'm always terrible in the warm-ups. In fact, the Bruins worry if I stop too many in the warm-ups. The thing about the warm-up is to get loose, get a little sweaty and feel the puck a little bit."

"I understand," I said.

"Remember, stand up. Going down is a reaction. You're less mobile. You've got to do your best to get up as soon as possible."

I gave a small groan . . . thinking of the laborious effort involved in hoisting myself up, rather—a friend of mine reported who had seen me at it—like a movie monster trying to pull himself out of a bog. . . .

Some of the players came by to pass the time—some to offer encouragement, others to pass on a quip: "Cherry has a surprise for you. A big one. You're staying in for the whole game."

No one else seemed at all perturbed. "That shouldn't surprise you," one of the Bruins said to me. "There's nothing you can do except carry on. I mean they all knew what Rocky Marciano was going to do to them."

"Well, thanks a lot."

Finally the tension in the Bruins' locker room began to settle in. The sticks lay in front of each player, fanning out into the room. The constant sound was the rip of tape; the players applied the strips of it to their skate boot tops; they worked strips onto their sticks. Through the locker room door we could hear the organ playing out in the arena, and the distant and increasing murmur of the crowd. From time to time a thin, squeaky voice emerged from a squawk box on the wall: "ten minutes"—intruding periodically to count down the time the team was due back on the ice . . . such a sudden, foreign presence in the locker room that it broke the quiet concentration and ignited a number of exhortations from the more voluble of the Bruins. "Keep loose and tramp 'em!" someone called out. "Stick it to them." "Everybody work out there!" Bobby Schmautz made a series of loud racing car "vroom! vroom! vroom!" sounds, and from back in the toilet stalls one of the players produced a perfect imitation of a hen laying an egg. I sat glumly looking out into the room. The goalies flanked me on their stools. Cheevers leaned across and had some more last minute suggestions to make.

"The Flyers have two incredible cannons at the point— Bladon and Daily," he told me. "Look out for them. When MacLeish gets the puck, as he comes across the middle he cuts loose, usually high, a shot he can do in full stride. MacLeish and Leach will always shoot if they have half a chance, and remember they don't have to get set to shoot."

"Right."

"Bobby Clarke is so good at the face-off in your zone that you'll have to rearrange your stance in the nets." He stood up to show me how. "As for Dornhoefer, he'll jam you in the crease," he went on. "He's not supposed to touch you, but you'll think he's part of your uniform. Get rid of him. Crack him with your stick!"

"Crack him with my stick?"

"That's right. Chop him."

"Chop him. You expect me to chop Dornhoefer."

"Why not?"

"I can hardly lift my stick up. Much less chop anyone with it."

"Use both hands," Cheevers said. "The main thing is just to keep telling yourself what to do."

I could not resist asking Cheevers if *he* ever talked to himself out there on the ice.

"No." He laughed and said, "I'd be afraid I might answer! Hey," he said. "One more thing. If you catch the puck, try to drop it out of your glove so your defensemen can move it up the ice and kill the clock. Your sentence will be up sooner."

The others along the bench were grinning. Schmautz fell to his knees and offered up a mournful prayer on my behalf —pleading that I had sinned, but not so deeply as to be worthy of punishment by a Flyer slap shot. "Spare him that!" he cried, rolling his eyes at the ceiling.

Gilles Gilbert, who was assigned to play in the goal that night, pretended to drop a skate on his bare foot—incapacitating himself. "I can't go on," he called out. "Send in the new guy."

Cheevers said: "You've got to hope Kate Smith's not out there to sing the National Anthem." He was referring to the hefty singer from Philadelphia whose singing of "God Bless America" had been such an emotional catalyst during the championship years of 1974 and 1975. "If she is," Cheevers was saying, "you're in for a serious five minutes."

Someone called out, "Hey, Georgie, give them the Northland sandwich!"

"What's the Northland sandwich?"

"That's the brand name on your stick, for Chrissake . . . stick it in their teeth is what I'm saying!"

"Oh."

I clumped over and sat down next to Terry O'Reilly to

get away from the taunting. He seemed a lot more concerned than the others—grief-stricken and tormented. "I
hate these people," he murmured to me. "They took the
Stanley Cup away from us."

"Bastards," I said. I tried to work up some hatred, but
the thought of the Flyers in the locker room just a few doors
down the corridor, doubtless doing just what we were
doing—staring at the floor between the fans of their hockey
sticks, and working up *their* hatred for the Bruins—meant
so little to me; I knew nothing of them. I had not seen them
beat up on my friends; they had not scored a goal on me,
or embarrassed me . . . at least not yet. Perhaps by the end
of the evening I would work up some venom, but at the
moment they were simply a vague foreign presence, like
two dozen Finns. On the other hand, O'Reilly knew them
as people who had contributed to the little stitch marks on
his face and the deprivation of honors, money, winter after
winter of this—indignities suffered so that animosity slowly
built like adding charcoal to a fire until a torrent of heat was
the result. One wondered how these people ever calmed
down.

I went back to my seat next to Cheevers just as Don
Cherry called for our attention and began his pregame talk.

He lashed at us; his voice rose. "There's a full house out
there. Every jack one of them remembers the play-offs last
year when you beat them and they'll really be standing up
to you." His vocabulary was formidably peppered with
cusswords, which was odd since in ordinary conversation
with him there was little of this. It was as if the official
language of the peroration required this sort of embellish-
ment. He glared at us. "Take it to them! If they ever have
one of our guys down, I don't care about the third-man rule;
the rest of you be there to help him."

It crossed my mind that Cherry was pumping the team up

too much . . . at least for my own good . . . that the Bruins
would go out and "muck it up in the corners" so heartily
that the Flyers would begin to bristle and retaliate, perhaps
by shooting high and ringing a few zingers off the goaltender's melon.

Cherry kept railing at us. He said he didn't care if the
Bruins were getting beaten 15–0 in the first five minutes (he
looked grimly over at me as he said this) but he'd remember
every time a check was made along the boards. That was the
sort of pressure he wanted.

How many times had the Bruins heard these same
words?—subjected before every game to this appeal to be
physical, to go out and "muck it up in the corners." It was
the Bruins' trademark. It was essential to their success. It
was a simple principle: tough players got more room on the
ice, owned it, like lepers being avoided—and that was
worth any amount of finesse. Physical pressure was what
made one team dominate another. Peter McNab said that
it was possible to sense when the other team sagged under
pressure—the analogy he used was that of a wounded animal on the veldt weakening, and the predators knowing it,
and closing in—and the great pros especially could feel
when it was happening to the other team and then they
would increase the pressure. You never could be reminded
enough.

And that, too, was why Cherry kept emphasizing the
team togetherness, even urging the players to break the
third-man rule, which was that players could not break into
a fight between two opponents without incurring heavy
fines and penalties. The official wording for this is "entering
an altercation." The French-Canadians refer to a bench
clearing as a *bagarre générale.* The rules are very rough on
the *bagarre générale.* In theory, two linesmen can handle a
fight between two hockey players, but when seventeen men

from each team get on the ice with their gloves off, things tend to get really out of hand. It was rare, even with the Bruins, that this rule was broken, because the fines came out of one's own pocketbook . . . but to hear it so obviously flaunted in a locker room tirade made a player feel sacrosanct: he was being told he was one who was above the rules.

When Cherry had done, we had just a few minutes left. Bridgework was removed: when the teeth came out, the face took on a slightly different aspect, collapsing slightly, like the first twinge of an umbrella being closed. Cheevers leaned across from his stool. He looked very serious. He had one last thing he wanted me to remember. "Stand up! Stand up!" he said, meaning, of course, to remind me to keep myself aloft on the ice, that I was useless if I fell down. Under the stress of the moment I misunderstood him. I thought he was telling me, for some odd reason, to stand up there in the locker room. I shot up from my bench abruptly, towering over him on my skates, and looked down at him questioningly.

"Not in here, for God's sake," Cheevers said. "Out on the ice." He shook his head. "A basket case."

Cherry read out the lines: Mike Forbes and Al Sims at defense, and the McNab line, with Dave Forbes and Terry O'Reilly at the wings, would start. He read out my name as the goaltender somewhat perfunctorily, I thought, making nothing of it in any jocular way, as if it were a perfectly natural choice to make, and then he looked over at me and said: "It's time. Lead them out."

I put on my mask and clumped to the locker room door. I had forgotten my stick. Someone handed it to me. I was the first Bruin in the tunnel. I could hear the Bruins beginning to yell behind me as we started out.

The tunnel to the rink is dark, with the ice right there at

its lip, so that one flies out of it, like a bat emerging from a cast-iron pipe, into the brightest sort of light—the ice a giant opaque glass. The great banks of spectators rose up from it in a bordering mass out of which cascaded a thunderous assault of boos and catcalls. Cherry was right. The Bruins were not at all popular in Philadelphia.

We wheeled around in our half of the ice . . . the Flyers in theirs. There was no communication between the two teams; indeed, the players seemed to put their heads down as they approached the center line, sailing by within feet of each other without so much as a glance. Seaweed had told me: "In hockey you don't talk to the guys from the other team at all, ever. You don't pick him up when he falls down, like in football." He told me about a pregame warm-up in the Soviet–Canada series in which Wayne Cashman had spotted a Russian player coming across the center line to chase down a puck that had escaped their zone; Cashman had skated over to intercept him and checked him violently into the boards. "Well, the guy was in the wrong place," Seaweed said when I expressed my astonishment. "He should have known better."

I skated over to the boards, working at the clasp at my chin to adjust my mask. The fans leaned forward and peered in at me through the bars of the mask—as if looking into a menagerie cage at some strange inmate within. "Hey, lemme see." A face came into view, just inches away, the mouth ajar, and then it withdrew to be replaced by another, craning to see. I could hear the voice on the public address system announcing me as the goaltender for a special five-minute game. The Bruins were motioning me to get in the goal. We were a minute or so away. I pushed off the boards and reached the goal in a slow glide, stopping, and turning myself around slowly and carefully.

The three officials came out onto the ice. The organist

was playing a bouncy waltzlike tune that one's feet tapped to almost automatically, but I noticed the officials pointedly tried not to skate to its rhythm as they whirled around the rink to warm up, perhaps because they would seem to demean their standings as keepers of order and decorum if they got into the swing of the music. They too came up and inspected me briefly, glancing through the bars of my mask without a word and with the same look of vague wonder that I had noticed from the fans.

The Bruins began skating by, cuffing at my pads with their sticks as they passed. Tapping the goaltender's pads is perhaps the most universal procedure just before the game —in most cases, of course, a simple gesture of encouragement, like a pat on the back, but in other instances a most distinctive act of superstition. The Buffalo Sabres had a player, Ric Seiling, their rightwing, who had it fixed in his head that things would go badly if he were not the last of the starters on the ice to top the goaltender's pads. The trouble was that the Sabres had another player, a big defenseman, Jerry Korab, of exactly the same inclination. On one odd occasion Bill Inglis, the Sabres' coach, put both men on the ice to start the game; the two of them, as the other players got set, began wheeling around the net, tapping the goaltender's pads, one after the other, to be sure to be the last before the puck was dropped—a sight so worrisome that Inglis made a quick substitution and got one of them out of there.

For me, even as I wobbled slightly in the crease from the impact of some of the stronger blows from my Bruin teammates as they skated by, I felt a surge of appreciation and warmth towards them for doing it. Two of the Bruins stopped and helped me rough up the ice in front of the cage —this a procedure so the goalie gets a decent purchase with his skate blades. Invariably, it is done by the goalie himself

—long, scraping side thrusts with skates to remove the sheen from the new ice. It occurred to me later that to be helped with this ritual was comparable to a pair of baseball players coming out to help a teammate get set in the batter's box, kneeling down and scuffing out toe-holds for him, smoothing out the dirt, dusting his bat handle, and generally preparing things for him, as if the batter were as unable to shift for himself as a store-front mannequin. However odd this may have appeared from the stands—the three of us toiling away in front of the net—it added to my sense of common endeavor. "Thank you, thank you," I murmured.

Other Bruins stopped by while this was going on, and peering into my mask they offered last-minute advice. "Chop 'em down! Chop 'em down!" I looked out at Bobby Schmautz and nodded. His jaw was moving furiously on some substance. "Chop 'em down!" he repeated as he skated off. Slowly the other Bruins withdrew, skating up the ice toward the bench or their positions to stand for the National Anthem.

I spent the anthem (which was a Kate Smith recording rather than the real article) wondering vaguely whether my face mask constituted a hat, and if I should remove it. My worry was that if I tampered with any of the equipment I might not have it in proper working order at the opening face-off. The puck would be dropped . . . and the Flyers would sail down the ice towards a goal-tender who would be standing bare-headed, face down, fiddling with the chin strap of his mask, his big mitt tucked under his arm to free his fingers for picking at the clasp, his stick lying across the top of the net . . . no, it was not worth contemplating. I sang loudly inside my mask to compensate for any irreverence.

A roar went up at the anthem's conclusion—something grim and anticipatory about that welter of sound, as if, Oh my! we're really going to see something good now, and I

saw the players at the center of the rink slide their skates
apart, legs spread and stiff, their sticks down, the upper
parts of their bodies now horizontal to the ice—a frieze of
tension—and I knew the referee in his striped shirt, himself
poised at the circle and ready for flight once he had dropped
the puck, was about to trigger things off. I remember thinking, "Please. Lord, don't let them score more than five"—
feeling that a goal a minute was a dismaying enough fate to
plead against to a Higher Authority—and then I heard the
sharp cracking of sticks against the puck.

For the first two minutes the Bruins kept the play in the
Flyers end. Perhaps they realized that a torrid offense was
the only hope of staving off an awkward-sounding score.
They played as if the net behind them were empty . . . as
if their goalie had been pulled in the last minute of a game
they had hoped to tie with the use of an extra forward. I saw
the leg-pad of the Flyers goaltender fly up to deflect a shot.

Well, this isn't bad at all, I thought.

There can be nothing easier in sport than being a hockey
goalie when the puck is at the opposite end. Nonchalance
is the proper attitude. One can do a little housekeeping,
sliding the ice shavings off to one side with the big stick.
Humming a short tune is possible. Tretiak, the Russian
goaltender, had a number of relaxing exercises he would
put himself through when the puck was at the opposite end
of the rink. He would hunch his shoulder muscles, relaxing
them, and he's make a conscious effort to get the wrinkles
out of his brow. "To relax, pay attention to your face. Make
it smooth," he would add, the sort of advice a fashion
model might tend to.

It is a time for reflection and observation. During a static
spell, Ken Dryden from the Montreal goal noticed that the
great game clock that hung above the Boston Garden was
slightly askew.

With the puck at the other end, it was not unlike (it occurred to me) standing at the edge of a mill pond, looking out across a quiet expanse at some vague activity at the opposite end almost too far to be discernible—could they be bass fishing out there?—but then suddenly the distant, aimless, waterbug scurrying becomes an oncoming surge of movement as everything—players, sticks, the puck—starts coming on a direct line, almost as if a *tsunami,* that awesome tidal wave of the South Pacific, had suddenly materialized at the far end of the mill pond and was beginning to sweep down toward one.

"A tsunami?" a friend of mine had asked.

"Well, it *is* like that," I said. "A great encroaching wave full of things being borne along toward you full tilt— hockey sticks, helmets, faces with no teeth in them, those black, barrel-like hockey pants, the skates, and somewhere in there that awful puck. And then, of course, the noise."

"The noise?"

"Well, the crowd roars as the wings come down the ice, and so the noise seems as if it were being generated by the wave itself. And then there's the racket of the skates against the ice, and the thump of bodies against the boards, and the crack of the puck against the sticks. And then you're inclined to do a little yelling yourself inside your face mask —the kind of sounds cartoon characters make when they're agonized."

"Arrrgh?"

"Exactly. The fact is it's very noisy all of a sudden, and not only that, but it's very crowded. You're joined by an awful lot of people," I said, "and very quickly. There's so much movement and scuffling at the top of the crease that you feel almost smothered."

What one was trained to do in this situation (I told my friend) was to keep one's eye on the puck at all costs. I only

had fleeting glimpses of it—it sailed elusively between the
skates and sticks as shifty as a rat in a hedgerow: it seemed
impossible to forecast its whereabouts . . . my body jumped
and swayed in a series of false starts. Cheevers had explained to me that at such moments he instinctively under-
stood what was going on, acutely aware of the patterns
developing, to whose stick the puck had gone, and what the
player was likely to do with it. The motion of the puck was
as significant to him as the movement of a knight on a chess
board. His mind busied itself with possibilities and solu-
tions. For me, it was enough to remember the simplest of
Cheever's instructions: "Stand up! Keep your stick on the
ice!"

The first shot the Flyers took went in. I had only the
briefest peek at the puck . . . speeding in from the point off
to my right, a zinger, and catching the net at the far post,
tipped in on the fly, as it turned out, by a Philadelphia
player named Kindrachuk, who was standing just off the
crease. The assists were credited to Rick Lapointe and Barry
Dean. I heard this melancholy news over the public address
system, just barely distinguishing the names over the uproar
of a Philadelphia crowd pleased as punch that a Bruins team
had been scored on, however circumspect and porous their
goaltender.

Seaweed had given me some additional last minute tips
at training camp on what to do if scored upon. His theory
was that the goaltender should never suggest by his actions
on the ice that he was in any way responsible for what had
happened. The goalie should continue staring out at the
rink in a poised crouch (even if he was aware that the puck
had smacked into the nets behind) as if he had been
thoroughly screened and did not know the shot had been
taken. In cases where being screened from the shot was
obviously not a contributing cause of the score, Seaweed

suggested making a violent, abusive gesture at a defenseman, as if that unfortunate had made the responsible error.

When the Flyer goal was scored, I had not the presence
or the inclination to do any of the things Seaweed had
recommended. I yelled loudly in dismay and beat the side
of my face mask with my catching glove. I must have
seemed a portrait of guilt and ineptitude. "I didn't see the
damn thing!" I called out. As I reached back to remove the
puck, the thought pressed in on my mind that the Flyers had
scored on their very first attempt—their shooting average
was perfect.

What small sense of confidence I might have had was
further eroded when soon after the face-off following the
Philadelphia goal, one of the Bruins went to the penalty box
for tripping; the Flyers were able to employ their power
play, and for the remainder of the action, the puck stayed
in the Bruins zone.

I have seen a film taken of those minutes—in slow motion
so that my delayed reactions to the puck's whereabouts are
emphasized. The big catching mitt rises and flaps slowly
long after the puck has passed. There seems to be a near-
studied attempt to keep my back to the puck. The puck hits
my pads and turns me around, so that then my posture is
as if I wished to see if anything interesting happened to be
going on in the nets behind me. While the players struggle
over the puck, enticingly in front of the crease, the camera
catches me staring into the depths of the goal, apparently
oblivious of the melee immediately behind me.

The film also shows that I spent a great deal of the time
flat on the ice, alas, just where Cheevers and Seaweed had
warned me not to be. Not much had to happen to put me
there—a nudge, the blow of the puck. Once, a hard shot
missed the far post, and in reaching for it, down I went, as
if blown over by the passage of the puck going by. The film

shows me for an instant grasping one of my defensemen's legs, his stick and skates locked in my grasp, as I try to haul myself back upright, using him like a drunk enveloping a lamppost.

Actually, my most spectacular save was made when I was prostrate on the ice . . . the puck appearing under my nose, quite inexplicably, and I was able to clap my glove over it. I could hear the Bruins breathing and chortling as they clustered over me to protect the puck from being probed out by a Flyer stick.

What was astonishing about those hectic moments was that the Flyers did not score. Five of their shots were actually on goal . . . but by chance my body, in its whirligig fashion, completely independent of what was going on, happened to be in the right place when the puck appeared.

A friend, who was observing from the seats, said the highest moment of comic relief during all this was when one of the Flyers' shots came in over my shoulder and hit the top bar of the cage and ricocheted away.

"What was funny," my friend said, "was that at first there was absolutely no reaction from you at all—there you were in the prescribed position, slightly crouched, facing out towards the action, stick properly down on the ice and all, and then the puck went by you, head-high, and went off that cross-bar like a golf ball cracking off a branch; it wasn't until four or five seconds, it seemed, before your head slowly turned and sneaked a look at where the puck had . . . well . . . *clanged*. It was the ultimate in the slow double-take."

"I don't remember," I said. "I don't recall any clanging."

"Hilarious," my friend said. "Our whole section was in stitches."

Then, just a few seconds before my five-minute stint was up, Mike Milbury, one of the Bruins defensemen out in front of me, threw his stick across the path of a Flyers wing coming down the ice with the puck. I never asked him why. Perhaps I had fallen down and slid off somewhere, leaving the mouth of the net ajar, and he felt some sort of desperate measure was called for. More likely, he had been put up to it by his teammates and Don Cherry. Actually, I was told a *number* of sticks had been thrown. The Bruins wanted to be sure that my experience would include the most nightmarish challenge a goaltender can suffer . . . alone on the ice and defending against a shooter coming down on him one-on-one. The penalty shot!

At first, I did not know what was happening. I heard the whistles going. I got back into the nets. I assumed a face-off was going to be called. But the Bruins started coming by the goal mouth, tapping me on the pads with their hockey sticks as they had at the start of things, faint smiles, and then they headed for the bench, leaving the rink enormous and stretching out bare from where I stood. I noticed a huddle of players over by the Philadelphia bench.

Up in Fitchburg I had been coached on what the goaltender is supposed to do against the penalty shot . . . which is, in fact, how he maneuvers against the breakaway: as the shooter comes across the blue line with the puck, the goaltender must emerge from the goal mouth and skate out toward him—this in order to cut down the angle on the goal behind him. The shooter at this point has two choices: he can shoot, if he thinks he can whip the puck past the oncoming, hustling bulk of the goaltender, slapping it by on either side, or he can keep the puck on his stick and try to come *around* the goalie; in this case, of course, the goalie must brake sharply, and then scuttle backwards swiftly, always maneuvering to keep himself between the shooter and the goal mouth. I would always tell Seaweed or Cheevers, whomever I was chatting with about the penalty shot, that

I had to hope the shooter, if this situation ever came up, did not know that I was not able to stop. All the shooter had to do was come to a stop himself, stand aside, and I would go sailing by him, headed for the boards at the opposite end of the rink.

Penalty shots do not come up that often. Gump Worsley in his twenty-one-year career had only faced two, both of which he was unsuccessful against—not surprising perhaps because the goals came off the sticks of Gordie Howe and Boom-Boom Geoffrion. But Seaweed had told me—despite the Gump Worsley statistics—that he thought the chances favored the goaltender . . . that by skating out and controlling the angle the goalie could force the shooter to commit himself. Also, he pointed out that since the shooter was the only other player on the ice, the goaltender always had a bead on the puck, whereas in the flurry of a game he had often lost sight of it in a melee, or had it tipped in by another player, or passed across the ice to a position requiring a quick shift in the goal. Others agreed with him. Emile Francis believed that the goaltender should come up with a save three times out of five. He pointed out while the goaltender is under considerable pressure, so is the other fellow—the humiliation of missing increased because the shooter *seems* to have the advantage . . . the predator, swift and rapacious, swooping in on a comparatively immobile defender. The compiled statistics seem to bear him out. Up until the time I joined the Bruins, only one penalty shot out of the ten taken in Stanley Cup play has resulted in a score —Wayne Connelly's of the Minnesota North Stars in 1968 off Terry Sawchuck.

The confidence that might have been instilled by knowing such statistics was by no means evident in my own case. I stood in the cage, staring out at the empty rink, feeling lonely and put upon, the vast focus of the crowd narrowing on me as it was announced over the public address system that Reggie Leach would take the penalty shot. Leach? Leach? The name meant little to me. I had heard only one thing that I could remember about him from my resume of Flyers players, which was that he had scored five goals in a play-off game, a record. I dimly recalled that he was an Indian by birth. Also a slap shot specialist . . . just enough information to make me prickle with sweat under my mask.

I gave one final instruction to myself—murmuring audibly inside the cage of my face mask that I was not to remain rooted helplessly in the goal mouth, mesmerized, but to launch myself out toward Leach . . . and just then I spotted him, moving out from the boards, just beyond the blue line, picking up speed, and I saw the puck cradled in the curve of his stick blade.

As he came over the blue line, I pushed off and skated briskly out to meet him, windmilling my arms in my haste, and as we converged I commited myself utterly to the hope that he would shoot rather than try to come around me. I flung myself sideways to the ice (someone said later that it looked like the collapse of an ancient sofa), and sure enough he *did* shoot. Somewhat perfunctorily, he lifted the puck and it hit the edge of one of my skates and skidded away, wide of the goal behind me.

A very decent roar of surprise and pleasure exploded from the stands. By this time, I think, the Philadelphia fans thought of me less as a despised Bruin than a surrogate member of their own kind. The team identification was unimportant, for an instant. I represented a manifestation of their own curiosity if they happened to find themselves down there on the ice. As for the Bruins, they came quickly off the bench, scrambling over the boards to skate out in a wave of black and gold. It occurred to me that they were coming out simply to get me back up on my skates—after all, I was flat out on the ice—but they wore big grins: they pulled me up and began cuffing me around in delight, the big gloves smothering my mask so I could barely see as in a thick joyous clump we moved slowly to the bench. Halfway there, my skates went out from under me—tripped up perhaps or knocked askew by the congratulatory pummels —and once again I found myself down at ice level; they hauled me up like a sack of potatoes and got me to the bench. I sat down. It was a very heady time. I beamed at them. Someone stuck the tube of a plastic bottle in my mouth. The water squirted in and I choked briefly. A towel was spread around my shoulders.

"How many saves?"

"Oh, twenty or thirty. At least."

"What about that penalty shot?"

"Leach is finished. He may not play again. To miss a penalty shot against you? The Flyers may not recover."

I luxuriated in what they were saying.

"Is that right?"

But their attention began to shift back to the ice. The game was staring up again. The sound of the crowd was different: full and violent. I looked up and down the bench for more recognition. I wanted to hear more. I wanted to tell them what it had been like. Their faces were turned away now.

10

I felt a tap on the back. An executive from *Sports Illustrated* was standing there. He asked if I would mind making a few remarks to an executive group who had come down from New York as guests of the magazine to watch the game. He would guide me back to where they were waiting. I took off my skates and pads, dropping them off in the locker room, and we walked back to a place called the Ovation Room, a fancy bar in the innards of the Spectrum approached by a maze of corridors. I padded along in my stocking feet. The place was dark and very well appointed, plush armchairs and dark mahogany tables. When I walked in, it took my eyes some squinting to adjust. The executives were seated around three or four tables pulled together in a special section—about twenty of them. I was offered a beer. It was cold and excellent.

Standing facing them, I gave a short summary of what it had been like out there on the ice, what it was to see Leach coming across the blue line, how distant he had looked at first, and how he loomed up in the mesh of my mask as I wandered out of the goal mouth to meet him.

The questioning began. The executives wanted to know about the violence of hockey. Wasn't a lot of it faked?

Oh no, not at all. I told them how important hockey

players felt that intimidation was; I told them about "muck-ing it up in the corners," and how the players felt any physical edge gave them a considerable advantage.

Another beer arrived. I was feeling fine. Very expansive. Occasionally, I ventured the word "we" in reference to the Bruins . . . as in "we muck it up in the corners because. . . ."

They wanted to know what I saw out there—did I see Holmgren, Dornhoefer, Clarke. . . . I mentioned a phe-nomenon similar to my football experience with the Detroit Lions—that under stress I was surprised at how focused and narrow one's field of vision became . . . as if one were looking at the field of play down the length of a pipe. Professional players mentioned this—that peripheral vision became nonexistent; the head turns like the periscope of an ancient submarine. In the Spectrum my concentration on the puck, flitting amongst the sticks, was such that I had no idea who the stickhandlers were. Dornhoefer, the subject of so many pregame discussions, could indeed have spent those five minutes in the crease with me as I was warned he would. I would not have known.

I told my audience that I could barely distinguish be-tween Bruins and Flyers. Perhaps it was better that way. I might well have been frozen by the sight of someone sud-denly recognized—like a bird transfixed by a cobra. "My Lord, here's Dornhoefer right here in the crease with me." But as it was, very little out in front of me was identifiable or meant very much.

They asked me: "Why do you think Leach missed?"

"Well, I never asked him," I said. "After all, I was flat on my back. Perhaps he was being kind. I prefer to think, though, that he was somewhat shaken by the giant appari-tion that came out to meet him, teetering, the stick at an alarming and odd angle. Surely, he'd never seen anything like that on the ice before."

Behind me, people wandered in and out. What must they have thought—a hockey player in the opulent surroundings of the Ovation Room. At first glance seeing the great double zeroes on the back of the jersey, the bulk of the hockey pants, and the bright socks, they could well have assumed that I was a portable representation of a hockey player, trundled in to be set up as an adornment to the decor of the bar. When they heard me speaking, some of them stayed and listened.

What none of us knew—as I addressed myself to such questions as those on violence—was that one of the worst brawls in the history of the NHL had suddenly broken out on the ice, just two or three walls and a few corridors from where we were standing.

It had started with a stick-jabbing joust between Wayne Cashman and a Flyers defenseman named Jim Watson. No sooner was this calming down, when Paul Holmgren, one of the more aggressive of the Flyers, went after Cashman and after a wild tussle the two of them were banished from the game. That was not the end of it. Under the stands, out of sight of the crowds, in the corridor outside the team locker rooms, which unfortuitously were adjacent to each other, the two went at each other again. Holmgren said subsequently that he thought Cashman was going to clobber him with his hockey stick—"gouge his eyes," as he put it. So he kicked at him with a skate.

One of the witnesses was a young locker room attendant who gave a vivid impression of what it was like to be caught in a length of confined hallway with two hockey players flailing at each other. "When I saw Holmgren's leg fly up and the fight start—the skates crashing on the concrete—I crouched down and got the hell out of there into one of the dressing rooms, hoping like hell they wouldn't follow me in there. If they came, still fighting, I was going to leap up on the row of lockers. Either that, or I was going to hide in the toilet stalls."

Out on the ice, the game had started up again. But then both the Bruins and the Flyers benches got word of the fracas going on back in the corridors and the benches emptied. It must have been puzzling to the Spectrum fans— seeing the players from both sides skating hellbent for the tunnels leading to the locker room. What could they have thought—suddenly looking down on players streaming from the arena as if they had word of a huge bomb under center ice.

Back in the corridors was not a place to be, Harry Sinden, the Bruins' general manager, told me later. "I was in the middle, but I wasn't tossing punches. I was trying to break things up and hoping I didn't get killed."

The overriding sound, to go along with the cursing and the heavy grunting of players pushing at each other, was the shriek of skate blades against the raw concrete floors of the corridor. All of this erupted at 4:56 of the second period of the game.

When the corridors were finally cleared, and the game started up again (with players going back to the locker rooms to sharpen their skate blades, dulled by contact with the concrete), suddenly at 8:06 of the period Terry O'Reilly cross-checked Orest Kindrachuk (could it have been because he had scored on me?) in the corner violently enough to start a fight between *these* two; a tremendous brouhaha broke out, with once again both benches emptying onto the ice, as if frustrated by the pushing and heaving in the confines of the corridors they were now going to truly vent their feelings at each other on every sector of the rink; the fray went on through different stages of vehemence for twenty-five minutes, and when it was done, eighteen players from the clubs were ejected from the game.

The referee, a harried man named Wally Harris, meted out
266 penalty minutes, 121 to Boston. This is not quite a
record—406 minutes in a game between Minnesota and
Boston in 1981 is—but afterwards hardly enough players
on the respective benches were there to make up two lines
to send out on the ice. Not counting the goaltenders the
Bruins had eight available players, the Flyers nine.

All during this, and, of course, unaware, I had been
sipping my beer in the Ovation Room. I said good-bye to
the executives—explaining that it had been pleasant talking
to them, but that I felt I ought to get back to my teammates
on the bench. I padded back down the corridors in my
stocking feet.

On the way to the bench I could hear the hubbub in the
Bruins locker room as I passed the door. I remember being
surprised because I could hear the roar of the crowd out in
the arena and knew the game was going on. I walked in.
The Bruins who had been ejected were sitting along the
benches in front of the lockers, a number of them holding
ice packs to their bruises. I was aghast. "We looked for
you," someone called out. "Where were you when we
needed you?"

"I was down in the Ovation Room," I explained.

They told me about the fight. I stared at Wayne Cashman. I asked, "Why didn't someone come down and get
me?"

The laughter rose along the benches, presumably at the
concept of one of the Bruins rushing down the corridors
("For God's sake, get him quick—he's in the Ovation
Room"), his skates crashing against the concrete, to fetch
me out of the shadows of the cocktail lounge and hurrying
me back to the rink as if my appearance on the edge of the
ice, looming at the entrance of the tunnelway, the ultimate
goon, would, like the arrival of Achilles outside the walls

of Troy, throw fear and confusion into the ranks of the
Flyers.

I crept to a locker room bench and sat down. The Bruins
were in the euphoria of winding down from the battle—
each in turn describing what they remembered about what
had happened out there on the ice. For a while they had
been badly outnumbered. Fewer of the Flyers had damaged
skates. It takes about four minutes to get a pair of skates
sharpened on the machine. Thus, of the line of Bruins
waiting at the machine, those who returned piecemeal to
the rink each in turn ran into a cluster of Flyers waiting at
the mouth of the tunnel to jump them. Terry O'Reilly was
met by three Flyers and after a surging struggle he was
toppled to the ice at the bottom of a heap. The kinetic strain
must have been literally palpable in that pile-up. O'Reilly
looked up and said, "Guys, you can kill me. But you'd
better, because I know who you are, and I'll come back and
take care of each of you in turn." The pile remained motionless, like the quiver of a huge beeswarm, while all this
was digested, and nothing happened.

Much of the attention in the lockerroom was directed
toward Peter McNab. He had always been thought of by
Don Cherry—in his habit of comparing his players to dogs
—as "the Golden Retriever": good-looking, perfect tem-
perament, big, friendly, not an ounce of meanness, and with
very little urge to tangle. Although McNab was obviously
a valuable part of the Bruins offense—he was a forty-goal-a-
year scorer—he was not in the mold of a Don Cherry
player, who would be someone like Stan Jonathan: small,
scrappy, tough, a kind of human variation of Don Cherry's
terrier, Blue. But what happened in Philadelphia was that
McNab came flying down that terifying corridor into a
waiting clutch of Flyers and was really given no choice *except*
to fight. It was if a gentle nature had finally been pushed too

far; he was like the farmer who comes raging out of the
Quaker Meeting house in the motion pictures and takes on
the black-hat villains in the street. He not only defended
himself but threw such a series of crunching punches that
his reputation bloomed. It was unlikely that Don Cherry
would think of him as a Golden Retriever quite so often.

I sat there in the licker room absorbing all of this, melancholy, and feeling sorry for myself. I kept thinking, How
could I have missed all this? What a journalistic blunder to
have been chattering away in the Ovation Room! How was
I going to explain my absence to Seaweed?

As I sat there, shaken with disappointment, I tried to
visualize that would have happened if I had for some reason
cut my talk to the executives short and returned to the
bench in the middle of it all. I would have rushed to the
locker room for my skates, no doubt in my haste lacing
them up loosely so that I would have made my appearance
at the tunnel entrance with my skates flopped over, my
ankle bones just barely off the ice as I sashayed out to find
the opposing goaltender.

That was the procedure, wasn't it? When the benches
cleared you *had* to go and "waltz." I remember Cheevers
telling me that he would lumber gloomily off the bench
knowing he was going to be fined by the League for doing
so, and certainly not keen on fighting anyone anyway
(". . . I'm not sure I can lick my lips") and he would start
out slowly to look for an opposing goalie. On one occasion,
when a bench-clearing episode occurred in a game against
the Buffalo Sabres—the *bagarre générale*—Cheesie skated
out and found Joe Daley, the Buffalo goalie; as they waltzed
around amongst the empty gloves of the more serious com-
batants, hands gripping the other's shoulders, each asked
the other how he was and what he was up to, and what his
plans were for the summer, and the family and everything,

and all the while knowing that for leaving the bench and passing these pleasantries out on the ice the League would fine them both three hundred dollars.

Don Cherry came by my bench. "I was sorry I wasn't out there," I said to him. "Truly."

"Well, you shouldn't be," Cherry said. "You'd have fallen down and the Flyers would have jumped you. Just like that. If a player falls down during a brawl, it's assumed he's fighting—why else would he fall down? I mean those guys out there just don't know about people who fall down because they're inadequate on skates."

"You mean like me."

"That's right. You'd fall over by mistake and some guy wouldn't be able to resist climbing on."

"Oh."

"You were very lucky out of it."

"I guess so."

"Besides, if you'd been hit, you would have bled all over the guy."

I started to dress. I noticed that the room had quieted down and the Bruins were looking over. I discovered why. They had carved up my clothing—my tie was chopped in half, the toes had been snipped from my socks, the seat was gone from my underpants . . . and as I pulled on these ruined items, the Bruins rocked back and forth in their stalls, pounding their ice packs on the wooden seats, and roared with laughter.

Don Cherry looked on. "Well, you've been initiated," he said. "It's a good thing you didn't lose your head of hair along with the bottom half of that tie. The hair usually goes too."

He watched me carefully knot what was left of my tie. "Well, you've had enough happen to you today," he said. Perhaps he was aware that I was still thinking about missing the fight. "You survived five minutes in the goal—including a big Flyers power play. You got the bottom of your underpants cut out. You gave a big speech in the Ovation Room . . ."

I grimaced.

". . . you stopped Reggie Leach's penalty shot."

"That's right."

"You've got enough to remember."

"Of course."

"You can always start with why you got your tie cut in half with a scissors."

"Absolutely," I said. "I intend to wear it once a week."

11

ONE of the consequences of playing even briefly with the Boston Bruins was, of course, that I became a strong supporter of the team. I opened the newspapers anxiously and read about them in the sports pages. I occasionally went up to Boston to see them play. When they came to Madison Square Garden I would get a pair of seats and sweat through their games.

It was quite a change from going to games before I joined the Bruins. Back in those days I often went to see the Rangers with a young woman, not a great hockey fan, for whom the best part of the game was between the periods. She enjoyed watching the cleaning of the ice. I did not mind. She was attractive. The evenings were very low key.

The buzzer would go off, signaling the end of the period, and sometimes I'd say, "Let's go on out back and have a beer." She would say, "No, no, I want to watch this." So we would sit there—the two of us, just about the only people in the arena—and watch the machines come out and clean the ice. The Zambonis. I suppose this appealed to some housewifely instinct in her. I never had enough courage to ask. The best time for her was when there was one long last strip of snow down the middle, and when the Zamboni had removed it and the rink glowed in this blue, pristine way she would sit there in her seat and gloat with pleasure. She also liked the elderly Garden employees who skated out on wobbly ankles and took the goals out to clear the way for the Zamboni and then set them back in afterward and housecleaned around the posts.

Then, of course, the wooden gate in the boards down at the end would open up and the players would come out and wheel around the ice to warm up for the next period. She'd pout and say, "Look, they're going to spoil it."

All of this was a kind of ritual. I enjoyed it. I even discovered some things to tell her about the Zamboni—that in Boston the man who ran the ice machine wore a fedora. He was considered quite a character, and got applauded when he made his entrance. The Bruins management eventually bought him a cowboy hat to give him a bit of extra flair. But the first time he wore it, while tipping it to the applause, it toppled off his head and fell under his machine.

In the Boston Garden there were others specialists backstage. When an egg was thrown, a specialist in egg removal came out. He also wore a fedora. He arrived with an ice scoop and a broom; he would clear the egg into a little pile, and then would leave the ice to fetch a shovel to carry off the egg pile. That was his ritual, and no amount of hooting at him for not bringing the shovel in the first place would get him to change it.

The girl liked the story about the egg specialist. "Will you take me to Boston?" she asked.

Sometimes the hockey we were there to watch seemed quite secondary. If there were questions, they were always the same ones when we sat down in our Garden seats—even if we had been to a game five nights before.

"Please, I'm sorry, but tell me about the blue lines . . . I promise never to ask again."

I cleared my throat. "There are two blue lines . . ."

"Yes, I can see them," she said.

". . . sixty feet in front of each goal. An attacking player coming down the ice cannot pass the puck across the blue line to a teammate before he crosses the line himself."

"Why?"

"It's called offside. There's a rule like it in soccer. It keeps players from lurking around the opposing goal mouth and waiting for long passes. They'd beat the goalie just about every time. Actually," I went on, "in the early days of hockey a player wasn't allowed to pass the puck forward at all . . . which meant that the attack moved very slowly. So the lines on the ice were actually introduced to speed the game up."

"Look at that woman's hat!"

"You're not going to ask me to try to explain 'icing,' are you?"

"You tried once, and got angry. Please. When are the Zambonis coming?"

"Quite soon. So to sum up . . ."

"Why are you always 'summing up'?"

". . . you're not allowed to precede the puck across the blue line. Nor are you allowed to pass the puck across two lines. If you do, the whistle blows and the puck is brought back to the circle in the zone where the pass originated and there's a face-off."

"The Zambonis are about to come," she said brightly. "They remind me of elephants. They should trumpet when they come out."

After my experience with the Bruins, however, this all changed. Perhaps she did not enjoy her evenings as much. We arrived at our seats very early—so I could watch the pregame warm-ups and point out the Bruins to her. "Look, there's Wensink, the enforcer! Makes doll houses. With little light switches inside . . ."

"Where?"

"That one there . . . the one with the huge Cossack moustache. That's Brad Park . . . over there." I pointed. I told her that one of the reasons he was so shifty on the ice was that there was a tree in his flooded-over backyard which he was forced to avoid when he was growing up in Ontario."

"Oh yes."

"Look! There's Wayne Cashman. Big eater of Chinese food!" I shouted to her. "The Bruins say that if he were ever in jail, he'd use his dime to order up a big meal from a Chinese take-out counter," etc., etc.

After the teams had left the warm-up drills for their locker rooms she had an extra chance to see the Zamboni because it came out then and did its work. Formerly we would arrive in the middle of the first period.

"Why are you so nervous?"

"The teams are about to come out."

"I've never seen you so skittish."

"They're listening to the pregame oratory at this very moment."

During the game itself I must have been a difficult person to sit beside. A lot of body English. Goals scored by the Rangers produced abrupt cries as if the puck had hit my ribcage rather than the back of the Boston net. The goals scored by the Bruins resulted in a lunatic euphoria, arms flung aloft. All of this was carried on in the midst of spectators who were rooting as rabidly for the Rangers as I was for the Bruins. She would warn me about getting out of control. "You're being looked at," she said. After a period was done she began asking if we could go to the corridors out back and have a beer. She needed some refreshment after the pressures of sitting there.

"Don't you want to watch the Zamboni?"

When the game was over, I would go down to the locker room to say hello to the team.

"I won't be long," I told her. "You can watch the Zamboni. And then after that, they begin melting the ice."

She said, "I'm warning you. I'm getting kind of bored with the Zambonis."

T H E year I played with them, the Bruins got into the Stanley Cup finals against the Montreal Canadiens. I saw three of the games. The Canadiens were favored. They had home-ice advantage. I remembered what Don Cherry had said about playing against them—that it was like maneuvering in the shadow of a big battleship . . . "always in the shadow of knowing how good they are."

I spent a couple of games in the press box where vociferous support of a team is very much frowned on. One is supposed to maintain an impartial attitude. In Montreal I was judiciously moved into a distant area, far up on a bank of seats, where my protestations and cries of support were not likely to annoy my fellow writers.

I missed the second game of the finals because of a commitment I had in New York City to act as auctioneer for an African Wildlife cause. The festivities were held in the Explorers Club. I stood on a raised platform at the end of the club's main room on the second floor. My mind wandered. I held up a painting of an elephant. "What do I hear for this rhino?"

Someone told me there was an ancient television set up in the club's Trophy Room on the top floor. Perhaps I could sneak up there to see what was going on. The top two floors were off-limits to the guests at the auction. An elderly club employee was standing by a velvet rope guarding the stairs to keep guests from wandering up there. When I was

spelled at the auctioneering, I bided my time and, creeping
by him when he wasn't looking, I scuttled up the stairs for
the Trophy Room. The place is a large, dim, vaulted attic
with animal heads adorning the walls, cabinets crowded
with strange artifacts from around the world, and as a cen-
terpiece on a long mahogany table stands a stuffed cheetah.
I could see the outline of his slim form in the gloom of the
street lights shining through the leaded panes. I found the
television set, and turned a large wooden knob. The screen
was an oval, like a portrait frame; the set took about a
minute to warm up; a small light glowed in its innards—I
checked behind to see, peering through a cardboardlike
grate—and suddenly the oval glowed with a blue-gray light
revealing the Bruins wheeling up-ice in double image, so
that each player was followed closely by a ghostly representation of himself. The rink seemed crowded with figures. It
did not bother me. I could distinguish which ones were the
Bruins, the patterns of their jerseys and I could hear what
the situation was: the teams were in overtime. I crouched
in the glow from the set and murmured encouragement. I
had only been there a few minutes when to my despair two
Guy Lafleurs, coming down the right wing, shot two pucks
at two Gerry Cheeverses, and both pucks flew into the goal
mouths.

I let out a lengthy, loud cry, a banshee wail that rever-
berated around the gloomy loft and down the stairs those
couple of flights to the ears of the man at the velvet rope.
I was told afterward that it gave him a jolt to hear that
sound; nothing was up there as far as he knew. His eyes
must have widened; he hurried down to see the club manager.

"There's something up in the Trophy Room!" he apparently announced.

They met me coming down the stairs. "Sir, the upper
rooms are closed."

I apologized. It would have been too complicated to explain about Lafleur's goal.

"I was looking at the trophies. The cheetah."

They stared at me, especially the gentleman who had been at the foot of the stairs and had heard the cry of woe. Could the sight of a stuffed animal have produced that awesome expression of grief?

For a few weeks after the loss of the sixth and final game in Boston I found myself wanting to aim sudden blows at inanimate objects.

"Why did you kick that trash container?"

"The Bruins. They lost the Stanley Cup."

"Did you hurt your foot?"

"Yes. Help me into that taxi."

I called up some of the Bruins to commiserate. They seemed to be taking it much more calmly than I was. Cheevers was in the hospital having some patchwork done on his right knee. His voice sounded cheerful over the phone. He wanted to talk about race horses, his great passion; he was starting a small stable. Why didn't I come up to Rockingham Park to try my hand at training one of them as a participatory journalism exercise. "It'll be easier than hockey," he said, "you won't fall down so much."

Terry O'Reilly seemed the most outwardly affected by what happened. He mourned his play in the Canadian series. "There are two levels of hockey," he told me. "One of them is to play okay and when you fire a shot at the goalie, you're just hitting it at him, and he may or may not stop the puck; the other level is when you go in and ring the shot off the net post and into the goal and the goalie is truly beaten. To do that, you have to rise above the norm . . . and that's what you have to do throughout the entire series when you play the Canadiens."

Mike Milbury, the second year defensemen, told me that right after the last game, which was in the Boston Garden,

he had headed for the little gym down the spiral staircase
to the floor below the clubhouse locker room. "It's quiet
and deserted down there," he said. "I don't like to sit up
there in the locker room cubicles and get interviewed. I'm
still too worked up about the game. If it's a silly question,
I'm irritated, and if it's a good question, I've still got my
mind on other things. So being useless in that sort of situation I try to get away. On the stairs down to the gym I met
Stan Jonathan. He had tears in his eyes. We hugged each
other . . . big bear hugs."

"What did you do afterwards?" I asked.

"Well, if you want to know," he said, "I tried to get
hammered. Actually that's a principle of mine after a loss—
get hammered early, out of the party, and home to bed. But
this time I couldn't. I tried to get hammered, but I kept
thinking of the key goals against us, especially when I was
on the ice and was involved. One of the things about hockey
is that for a goal to be scored someone must make at least
a small error. You can't discount the brillance of a particular
play, but usually the greatness of a great player is that he
can take advantage of a small error. I kept thinking about
Larry Robinson's goal in the fifth game of the series—
maybe the most crucial goal of the series. I got beat by him
one-on-one. I can recall exactly what went through my mind
—this frightening dialogue: should I hook him rather than
let him go by? Or trip him, and take the two-minute penalty. Both times the answer was no. Cheevers in the goal
was going to take care of the problem. 'Cheevers got him!'
my mind said, and of course I was wrong. That goal sapped
us. I think back on it a lot."

I wondered aloud if that instant would disappear along
with all the other moments of tribulation. I mentioned that
John Havlicek, the Celtics' great basketball star, finally
couldn't remember individual baskets, even the most cru-

cial ones, because they were so many that they seemed to flow together in a continuous, undefinable stream . . .

Milbury shook his head. "I can describe every goal in detail—and there must have been two-hundred of them—scored against us during the season, and certainly every goal scored when I was on the ice. It's like golfers. People are amazed when those professionals with great accuracy recall every shot, and its circumstances, over the course of a tournament. I think that's so with most hockey players—that they have amazing recall for goals. Sometimes I'll describe a goal to my wife that happened months before, and everthing about it. If you're a defensemen, as I am, very often the goal involves that small error I was telling you about . . . which makes it hard to forget and why you get hammered afterwards sitting on a bar stool. . . . "

What did the wives make of this tortured behavior? Mike Milbury's wife, Debbie, was very succinct about it. "The house would be quiet for days, especially after the play-offs. After losing a play-off we might not see our husbands for a week. We didn't particularly mind. Until they got themselves together, we didn't want them around."

The wives tended to think of this kind of behavior as peculiar to hockey. Carol Smith, Rick's wife, felt that it was a kind of macho ethic that derived from hockey's heritage being rooted in the Canadian frontier traditions. The game was far more male-oriented than other sports. There was never any question, for example, of traveling to an opposing team's city during the play-offs to watch. During the World Series, Carol—not without envy—would watch the baseball wives from both teams sitting in the sun in the stadium box seats, very often with their offspring, a baseball cap set oversized on their small heads, seated beside them. Nothing like that in hockey, or even the *thought* of it. She told me that when she and Rick were courting, she would follow him around the country on the road trips but always traveling on a different plane and inevitably staying somewhere else when in the city.

The telephone had always been the only link. On the road, the players would come back to the motel, exhausted, and call home. Wayne Cashman used to fall asleep talking to his wife on the phone. Esposito, his roommate, would hear Lynn's voice murmuring through the mouthpiece, chattering on about the horses (she was an excellent rider and the Cashmans kept horses) or the children, or whatever, the receiver perched on his roommate's shoulder, and after a while Esposito would lift off the phone and say into it, "Lynn, Wayne's asleep," and she'd swear a little and that would be the end of it.

I asked Carol Smith if the pressures were the same during the seasons—was it just as unrelenting?

"Whenever the team lost a game," Carol said, "socializing, even with a wife, was the last thing they had on their minds. You had to wait for them out in the corridor. Even the Bruin wives with the great fur coats waited out there. You had to get to the parking lot quick. No autographs out there. It broke my heart seeing some of those kids."

"What was the ride home like?"

"Rick would drive. Absolutely silent. The only words came when you reached home, got out of the car, shut the door, and went into the house. You said, 'Thanks for the ride.' "

12

FOR many of the wives, game night in Boston was a chance to dress up. Some did not bother about it, of course, but for others the ultimate symbol was a fur coat, the longer and thicker the better. Usually, the wife left her fur or stole in a small, rather dingy room under the stands called the Wives' Room, which had a guard at the door and was exclusively theirs. The trouble with wearing finery out to the seats themselves was that the clifflike properties of the Boston Garden invited a steady shower of detritus from above, very often a heavy spray of beer. The wives would arrive back in the Wives' Room with their hair damp and speckled with popcorn. During the play-offs when the balcony crowds were excessively rambunctious, the wives brought little hand umbrellas to their seats for use during boisterous moments above.

The most famous area of the loftier heights was a section inhabited by the Gallery Gods—"fans who were maniacs but lively" as Carol Smith described them. One season rather than suffer what came down from the Gallery Gods (not only liquid and various solids but invective of a particularly virulent sort with nothing like a barrier of glass to keep it from reaching ears below) she decided to watch a game or so in their company. "The first time I sat with these

Armenians. The noise up there was incredible. A lot of betting—who would score first, who would get in the first fight. I had a fine time up there. They gave me a Gallery Gods jacket."

Most of the Bruins wives have traditionally sat in a single row situated right above the goal which the opposing team defends twice during the game. Presumably the management assumes the wives would rather be closer to offensive rather than defensive action. It is known as "Wives' Row." It was often a strain sitting there. Debbie Milbury sat for a year next to Diane Gilbert, the goaltender's wife. Whenever the opposition began sweeping down on her husband in goal, Diane would grab hold of Debbie's arm and squeeze it, and when a shot on goal was taken, she would give Debbie's arm a ferociously hard nip. Debbie said she could barely lift her arm after the season was over. She was very fond of Diane, a lovely French-Canadian girl. "But I thought there had to be an easier way to watch hockey than that." So then next year she applied for seats away from Wives' Row.

"Actually I'm surprised that Diane sat in the Wives' Row," Debbie told me. "It was always the tradition, it was explained to me, for goaltenders' wives to sit away from everyone else. It is really too difficult a situation to deal with socially if your husband is a goalie and gets scored on. Especially missing a save he might have made. No one knows quite what to say."

I asked, "Was there ever any communication between you and Mike down on the ice . . . a wave?"

Debbie said, "The Wives' Row was right above the exit they'd go out at the end of the game and between the periods. Sometimes on the way out Mike would look up and wave. Everybody in our section would stand up, a couple of girls would shout, and everybody'd wave back—each thinking his wave was for them. Then when I moved from Wives' Row, sometimes I'd see his face looking over from where he was sitting on the bench. I often wondered what he must have thought—especially when he wasn't on the ice —because he'd see me yakking away with my friend, Rosemary. Going to the game was a big thing because it meant being away from the kids and the household for a time, so one could check on what was going on outside. I remember a friend of mine a couple of seats down looking back over her shoulder and trying to snap a photograph of the two of us watching the game. She couldn't. We were always looking at each other, gabbing. Of course, when Mike was on the ice, it was different. I'd watch. I used to wish that he'd do one great thing on the ice and then the coach would take him out and he wouldn't play for the rest of the night."

It was very much frowned on *not* to go to the game. Apparently Guy Lafleur's wife never came to a game (it was a fact known throughout the league); nor did Rogie Vachon's, or Guy Lapointe's. At Boston, this kind of *laissez-faire* attitude would be considered an affront to those who sat in the Garden and sweated it out. You *had* to be on hand to support the team.

It turned out there was a near symbiotic relationship between the fortunes of the team and the closeness of the wives. When the team was doing well, the wives were practically a family; in murkier days, the cohesiveness among the wives disappeared somewhat: charity events would fall apart; a young wife would have a baby shower and only a few would show up; half the guests would arrive at a dinner. Their moods reflected very much what their husbands went through when the team was doing badly.

If the team had lost, Carol Smith would very often not go back to the Wives' Room. "Too gloomy back there. If you waited in your seat for the players to come out of the

locker room you could watch the mice come out into the
deserted garden and sometimes the rats. They *knew!"* Carol
said. "They were conditioned to come out after the game
was over, the crowds were gone, and before the cleaners
came between the rows with their brooms. In fact, there
were mice in the Wives' Room. I used to imagine them
waiting in all those furs and stoles."

"Wow!" I exclaimed.

"It's true," Debbie said. "It's such an old building.
Sometimes during a game, if it had gotten out of hand, the
wives went back into the Wives' Room to play poker. If you
heard a shriek from back in there, it was not that someone
had picked up a full-house hand, but a mouse had run across
the floor. The wives at the table picked up their legs; they
were used to it."

I asked how the wives behaved when their husbands got
into fights—supposing that they would go slightly berserk
in Wives' Row.

"No," Carol Smith said. "When John Wensink fought,
I used to look down the line at Rhonda Wensink. I never
saw anything that made you think that she was watching
John down there. She never flinched. She stood up. She had
to stand up because everyone else did. It always made me
think how different they were off the ice. Maybe that
helped. John made doll houses. Terry O'Reilly would fight
and I never could forget that during the afternoon, just
hours before, he had been restoring furniture or working
on stained glass windows. It was someone else down there.
Someone you barely knew."

Betty Cheevers was never concerned by the fighting.
"You see it so often, you get used to it. What frightened
me more were the freak accidents . . . what skates do, and
the pucks. Gerry had five teeth knocked out the night his

son, Craig, was born. January twenty-fourth, nineteen sixty-
five. Not a date to forget. He had been on a road trip and
got off the bus at six A.M. He heard his son had been born
just after midnight . . . two and a half months early! He
rushed in to see me and then that night at the Garden—no
wonder after not having slept in over a day—he put his
glove up for an easy hand save and the puck curved in and
hit him on the mouth. The next morning he came to see me.
I could hardly recognize him. Battered. Swollen lips. He
could barely speak. Nothing but a big circle in his face when
he smiled. He got more attention from the nurses than
either Craig or me!"

I gave a low whistle. "I guess you never think it's going
to happen."

"It was the first time he ever lost anything to a puck,"
Betty said, "He'd been hit on the cheek a couple of times,
but nothing more."

"What happened to the famous mask Frosty Foristal
painted up?"

"I know one's in the Hall of Fame in Toronto. We have
one in the house. At least I think we do. It's in a coat closet,
as I recall, thrown back up there on a shelf. Isn't that *awful*.
It's the only momento he's got from all those years. Perhaps
we don't have it out because someone might take it."

I asked her about the poker games in the Wives' Room
Carol Smith had described. "It wasn't poker," Betty said.
"It was euchre, which is a favorite card game among
Canadians. Carol is American, so I guess she wouldn't
know. We'd drive into Boston with our husbands, usually
a couple of hours before game time, and then to kill time
we'd set up tables in the Wives' Room and play euchre. It's
an easy game, which is important because it means that you
can talk while you play."

"Is it true about the mice?"

"Oh yes. We'd lift up our feet and yell. Then we'd get back to the card game and our conversations."

The Wives' Room, despite its fauna, was very much a social center. It was where the wives waited for their husbands if the evening had gone well. The place was lively with conversation. The players would put their heads in the door. They were always immaculately dressed in coat and tie. On rare occasions someone would appear in the Wives' Room in a turtleneck. The Canadians tended to conform to a dress code far more formal than that of their southern neighbors; also it was a firm tradition in hockey: all the teams dressed in suits and ties when they went on the road.

Usually, the last player to peer in the Wives' Room was Gerry Cheevers. He was always the last player out of the locker room. "Maybe that was why he was so even-tempered no matter what had happened on the ice," his wife suggested. "He was in there for such a long time he could unwind. He was never moody or indifferent. Of course, you have to remember that this was not really much of a problem: the Bruins didn't lose very often."

After Cheevers had collected her, the pair often would join other Bruins couples at the Branding Iron, or in one of the restaurants up Route 1 on the way home to the North Shore. The place of the rendezvous would have been settled in the Wives' Room.

At first, Debbie Milbury was somewhat intimidated by the Wives' Room. She said of it: "There was a very established pecking order in there. As a new wife in 1975 I just went in there to leave my coat and then grab it after the game and run. We addressed the wives of the older players as 'Mrs.' even though—thinking back on it—they were, most of them, only in their late twenties. Then, of course, you got broken in, assimilated, and you felt as much a part of that group as Mike did being with the team."

Betty Cheevers felt that one of the reasons for the closeness of the wives was that none of them had outside interests; they were totally involved with their husband's hockey
careers. "We were there to see that there were no outside
pressures on them. We were all in that together. Also we
rented our houses and tended to go back to Canada in the
summers. So we never got to know our neighbors. That
made us very dependent on each other. It's very different
nowadays. The players buy their houses; their wives work
or go to school. The neighborhood becomes important.
These days a hockey player's wife is a very different social
being. Of course, part of it is growing up with the times."

When the team was on the road, everyone would gather
in one of the wives' homes to watch the game on television.
The "cat-pack," the players called the group—over twenty
of them, bringing their own dinner (usually with a surfeit
of cucumbers and dill pickles to keep the weight down),
and doing the dishes afterwards. The organizers were usually Rose Cherry, Betty Cheevers, or Lynn Cashman. The
wives perched around the living room or on the floor in
front of the television set. The radio was turned on in the
kitchen; in fact it provided the commentary for the entire
group, which preferred Bob Wilson, the radio broadcaster,
to his television confrères. The television sound was turned
off; Wilson's voice boomed through the house.

Not that the women kept their own voices to themselves.
Debbie Milbury told me that the girls learned to talk briskly
about whatever came into their heads while their eyes
stared straight ahead at the television in absolute compre-
hension of what was going on *there.* "Split personalities—
twenty or so of us. Actually it was better *not* to talk hockey,
because you had to be so careful. You could never bad-
mouth anyone, or even be critical. It would have destroyed

the closeness that was really remarkable about being a Bruins wife."

One evening Debbie Milbury was watching her husband on television in a game against the New York Rangers in Madison Square Garden. Her husband was a particular favorite of Don Cherry's—possessed of exactly the tough, feisty behavior that Cherry liked to think personified his Lunch-Pail Gang. The admiration was reciprocated. Milbury asked Cherry to act as godfather to his firstborn, Luke, and once, to his everlasting embarrassment, he announced to an interviewer on television, "I think so much of Don Cherry that I made him the father of my child."

The game Debbie was watching ended on a spectacular play by Boston. With just eight seconds to go with Boston ahead by a goal, Phil Esposito of the Rangers broke in on the goal, alone, practically as if a penalty shot were being taken. Gerry Cheevers made an amazing defensive maneuver which preserved a 3–2 win for the Bruins. When Debbie next looked at the television set, she saw an astonishing sight—her husband, Mike, far up in the stands assailing, along with Pete McNab, a massive fan who at one point launched a kick at her husband. "It's funny," she told me, "how even in fights you see personality traits that are distinctly your husband's." She saw Mike remove the fan's shoe and clobber him with it a few times. "Then I saw him take the guy's shoe, look at it, and I thought, 'Oh my God, what he's going to do is sling that shoe out onto the ice and let the guy walk home in his socks!' That's exactly what happened! What was interesting to me was seeing a personality trait in *public* that was so typical of him. I mean I just *knew* he was going to scale that shoe out there."

Eventually I was able to ask Milbury himself about the incident.

"Oh yes. It happened on December twenty-third, just

before Christmas when Cheesie stoned Espo, and we'd won the game. I was as happy as a clam. It's in your best interests in New York to get off the ice as soon as you can. In fact, being near the exit gate, I was the first Bruins player into the locker room. Next came Cheesie, sweating—because, as you know he was never in the best of condition—the steam pouring off him like a locomotive. He sat down with a big puff. But he was the last one in the locker room. *No one else came in.* I said, 'Cheesie, what's going on out there?' He said, 'I don't know. Something. But I'm not going back out.' "

"Like me in the Ovation Room," I suggested.

"Except," Mike said, "I went back out there and got involved in a six million dollar suit. Would that I had stayed in there like Cheesie. Or like you in the Ovation Room. The suit was eventually thrown out, but it took a long time. What happened was that I jogged on down the runway to see what was going on, and there at rinkside I found a lot of pushing and shoving going on and some of our guys up in the stands. Peter McNab was way up, maybe eight or nine rows. I found out later what had happened—that Al Secord had a problem with John Davidson; the battle had drifted over by the stands where a fan, a couple of brothers actually, had taken a whack at Stan Jonathan. In the course of things the fans had grabbed his stick. That sent a swarm of Bruins into the stands, headed by Terry O'Reilly, to get those responsible. McNab caught the guy who'd gotten the furthest away, a really massive guy. I had no idea at all what was going on, but I went up there to help. Peter had this guy pretty much under control, down across the seats, but he took a kick at me, as Debbie described, and that was when I wrenched this big shoe off his foot—a huge cheap penny loafer—and I whacked him with it a few times. It felt good to the touch. Whippy. Then I scaled it out over the

ice. What I'd done looked awful in the films . . . much worse
that it really was. They called me in to see it. 'Despicable.
Just despicable!' the president of the NHL kept saying. The
Bruins down in the lower seats who were really flailing
away with their fists, just slugging it out, got fined $500. I
got suspended for a few games. Maybe it was because the
shoe was so big. It looked like I was hitting him with a big
club."

13

THAT old adage about coaching that if the bus breaks down the thing to do is shoot the bus driver came to pass with the Bruins after two difficult seasons. Don Cherry was fired and the following year, Gerry Cheevers took over. I sent him a little note congratulating him and mentioning that I was prepared to come out of retirement if he needed me. I went to the games and watched him outfitted from a collection of sports coats walk back and forth behind his charges on the bench. The coats often looked as if they had been cut from the blankets his race horses wore at Rockingham Park.

Before my stint with the Bruins, the performance of hockey coaches during a game had always been something of an enigma. Watching them from my seat I often wondered what they actually *did,* especially compared to coaches in other sports who always seem to be so deeply involved in what is going on. Football coaches wear headphones; they confer with their assistants. They have even been known, as in the case of Woody Hayes, the former coach at Ohio State, to reach out across the sidelines and clothes-line an opposing player coming down the way. Baseball managers walk down to the end of the dugout and kick the water cooler. They get on the bullpen phone. Basketball coaches skid chairs out onto the court. I once saw K. C. Jones of the Boston Celtics leap up in anguish and come down with one foot in a bucket reserved for oranges; he wore it for a few splendid seconds. But hockey coaches seemed imbued with an immense calm. Impeccably dressed from what must be a vast wardrobe (a different display every night) they stand in back of their charges rather like a schoolmaster behind a boys' choir—detached, magisterial, aloof, pondering deep thoughts. Sometimes they lean forward to say something, but apparently think better of it. They stroke their chins, and look dreamily out over the heads of their players. Sometimes they take a little stroll down behind the bench, down and back.

After the Philadelphia game I asked Don Cherry about his wardrobe. I remembered for that game he wore a blazer, very tight-fitting trousers, highly polished shoes, a red tie, and a bright red handkerchief in his breast pocket.

"I always believed in being a sharp dresser behind the troops," Cherry said. "The guy before me, Bep Guidolin, wore a leather jacket, and I can remember when I turned up in a suit, vest, and so forth, for my first game coaching, Bobby Orr looked up and said, 'Hey, what about our *coach!*' I have about fifteen suits. Very sharp, tailored especially for coaching; they're so form-fitting and tight that I can't sit down."

"You mean you literally can not sit down."

"Exactly."

"How do you get to the Boston Garden?" I had a curious image of Cherry driving down from North Andover in some sort of van which allowed him to stand behind the wheel like a sea captain. Or perhaps he kept the trousers off, laid out stiff in the back seat, and drove down in his boxer shorts.

"I have a few of the suits there at the Garden," he told me. His procedure was to sit around in the locker room wearing a robe; when the team was out on the ice for its pregame warm-ups he took a shower; then, feeling all fresh and peppy, as he put it, he would squeeze himself into one of the suits.

"Selection is very important. They'd notice if you wear the same one twice in a row. Once, a woman came up to me and complained, 'Hey, you wore that one last month.' "

"What happens if you try to sit down?"

"It just can't be done," Cherry said. "It's a suit just for standing up. You might fall over, like a smokestack, but you couldn't sit down."

"You couldn't carry a wallet in the thing, or a pencil?"

"Are you kidding?" Cherry laughed. "Once I forgot to have a jacket there in the locker room, and I went around among the players' stalls looking for something that might fit. I finally chose Mike Milbury's. That night the TV broadcaster kept on mentioning the great-looking coat I was wearing. The cameras would pan over, and what I actually was wearing was practically a hand-me-down that Milbury had bought off the rack for $49.95!"

We began talking about pregame pep talks. I said I had admired the one he had given in Philadelphia, and also was unnerved by it—his appeal to us to ignore the third-man rule and rush onto the ice if a fight broke out.

"Yes, and where were you when it happened?"

I hit my forehead in mock dismay. "The Ovation Room! That damned Ovation Room," I moaned, "and having a cool beer . . . "

"Never mind. My speech couldn't have been all that great because we lost the game 6–2."

"Well, there were a lot of distractions," I said. "They probably forgot."

I asked if he had a particularly favorite pregame speech he could remember.

Cherry thought for a while. "Well, this one time I felt we needed some livening up. We were playing the Canadiens in a series and our team seemed dead—certainly compared to Montreal who were lively and shouting it up even during the pregame warm-ups. So I gathered the team together and I told them about Lord Nelson, how just before the Battle of Trafalgar he had appeared on deck and his men not only on board but from neighboring ships gave him a great cheer, *hip hip hooray!* The French heard this across the water, the cheering, and saw the throwing of hats in the air and all that, and it put them a bit on edge. So I told the guys that I wanted them out on the ice shouting and hollering during the warm-ups, especially when they were near the center-line, the red line, where the Canadiens on the other side could hear them. Well, the guys went out and did exactly that and eventually we won the game. After the last period was over, I came back into the locker room; there they were, all lined up, and they gave me a hip hip hooray! *Hip! Hip! Hooray!*"

"No one threw their hats?"

"No hats."

I asked: "Present company aside, who was the best you ever heard in this sort of pregame oratory?"

"The best motivator ever was Punch Imlach. He'd come in with this big wad of cash, maybe $2000, and throw it around the floor of the locker room. 'See that money!' he'd shout at us. 'Those other guys down the corridor are trying to pick your pockets of it . . .' etc. etc. Or he'd tap these three spikes into the wall with a hammer, just getting them started, speaking of them as 'nails in the other guys' coffin," and he'd stride around the locker room with this big hammer in his hand, talking about this, and when the first period was over and we'd troop back in with a one-goal lead or more, he'd step up and slam that first nail in all the way with his hammer. Same after the second period. It was hell on the locker room wall, but it was effective stuff."

"Suppose the other team had won one of those periods?" I asked.

"I think he would have come after *us* with his hammer," Cherry said.

The other Boston Bruin I talked to about coaching was Harry Sinden, the general manager, who had coached the team in the late sixties. He was also a strong proponent of active communication with the players.

"What about during the game?"

"I do a lot of talking from behind the bench," Sinden said. "I know a lot of great coaches who don't, but I find it essential."

"What sort of things do you say?"

"It's mostly a question of pointing out to the players what is going on out in front of them . . . either good or bad. 'Now that's the way it ought to be done.' 'Did you see that?' Or, 'No, no, that's wrong. Bad.' It's not pointing the finger at anyone in particular, showing him up, but explaining by example. It's much more meaningful to a player having something explained while it's going on out there on the ice than looking at a drawing on a blackboard."

"What about pregame oratory?" I asked. "Have you ever had a peroration go sour on you?"

"You can let the steam out so easily. I'll tell you one. In 1966, my first year of coaching the Bruins, the Montreal Canadiens came to town, to the Garden. They were the best in the league by far. At the time we had a weak team, in the basement, but at the end of the second period we were ahead 2–0 with a tremendous upset in the making. I wanted to win very badly. As we went into the lockerroom, I kept

wondering what I could say. I closeted myself in the little
coach's office and decided I'd come out and emphasize just
two points. Make it simple. The first thing I was going to
tell them was to keep up the strong fore-checking, really
going after the Canadiens as they came up the ice. The
second was not to take any foolish penalties and allow the
Canadiens power plays. So I walked out of the office and
said to them, 'Now I want to make two points. Pay attention. If you do exactly as I tell you, we're going to win this
game.'

"You can imagine how attentive they were. Not a sound.
So I stood in front of them and I said, 'The first thing I want
you to remember is don't take any foolish penalties! Right?
Now the second thing is . . .' and I couldn't *remember*. What
I wanted to say utterly vanished from my mind. Perhaps it
was because I had changed the order of what I wanted to
tell them and put the second point first. In any case, I
blurted out, 'Goddamn it, I've forgot it!' "

"What happened when you went back onto the ice?"

"I'm afraid it ended up a 2–2 tie. It was not what I had
in mind."

S I N D E N had stayed very much in the background
during my weeks with the Bruins. Occasionally I would see
him staring gravely through the glass at my maneuverings
on the ice. He had seen me perform in Philadelphia. Afterwards, when I went up to see a game at the Boston Garden,
I would always go up and say hello. Sometimes we would
go out and have a drink.

"Harry," I asked him one evening. "What if you could
put together a kind of composite hockey player—made up
of the best attributes of the various players you've watched
over the years." I told him I had done something of the sort

with a football acquaintance, Bill Curry, formerly with the Baltimore Colts. We created the perfect quarterback— using the best arm from one, the quick release of another, the motivational abilities of a third. I said, "We also created the world's 'worst' football player. He had Joe Scibelli's breath. Scibelli was a lineman with the Los Angeles Rams. Alex Karras had told me about him. Before the game he ate all sorts of garlic meals and used his breath with great effectiveness on the line of scrimmage in his rookie year until he could perfect his natural physical abilities."

Harry said he wasn't sure about constructing the "worst" composite, but the other interested him.

"Let's see. I guess you could start off with stick handling. If I had the opportunity to borrow that ability from anyone it would be Wayne Gretzky's—those soft, quick hands. He's almost impossible to check. He sees you coming with that incredible peripheral vision and he's gone, the puck with him. The theory is, ride him off the puck. But how are you going to bodycheck him? I've never seen him hit yet. It's been said the only way to do this might be when he's standing still singing a national anthem. Gordie Howe was a great stick handler too—he used to speak of his stick 'talking' to him, and 'seeing' with it. Gretzky has that kind of magic."

"It's not something you could say about John Wensink."

"No," Sinden said with a smile. "There are a small number of choices when you get control of the puck—whether to shoot, carry, or pass. All of these go through the mind of the average enforcer like John, but it's too much for them. They have their own priorities. So it shouldn't worry them that they haven't the slightest idea what to do with the puck. Dave Schultz never worried about the puck."

"The Hammer?"

"Right. He treated the puck about as badly as he treated

his opponents. When the puck came to him it looked like it was alive and something to beat to death. Bang it! Cut it!'' Sinden laughed. "Curiously,'' he went on, "some of the top scorers have not been at all deft at puck handling. Ken Hodge of the Rangers. A great shot. Great right wing. Scored fifty goals a year. Couldn't carry the puck three feet. Even Wensink scored twenty-eight goals one year.''

"How about speed?'' I asked.

"Yvon Cornoyer of the Montreal Canadiens was as good as anyone,'' Sinden said. "If he got a step on you, there was no way you would catch him. He had a curious skating style. Unlike most hockey players, who move from a standing start with three or four short, choppy strokes and then settle into a full-length stride, Cornoyer never went into a full-length stride at all. It always looked like he was running down the ice . . . in fact that was the name they hung on him—'The Road Runner.' He was short, 5'7'', with these tremendously powerful legs and great balance. It's odd, because putting together a composite I'd like to think I'd end up with a much taller player, six feet, with a full-length skating style—like a Gordie Howe. Or a Guy Lafleur. But for speed, sheer speed, you'd have to borrow the legs of the Road Runner.''

I asked, "Against Phil Esposito, say, what would the difference between them be if they raced the length of the rink?''

Sinden laughed. "Well, you haven't picked much in the way of an opposition. Esposito is by no means a fast man on the ice. In fact, in your composite of bad attributes he'd be a leading candidate for the worst skater.'' Sinden chuckled again and shook his head. "In Moscow he slipped on a rose petal from a bouquet which had been presented before the game and fell flat. He fell out of a penalty box his last year in the Juniors and broke a wrist. Well, in answer to your

question, I'd guess by the time Cornoyer reached the opposite boards, Esposito'd be coming up on the blue line
. . . but that's not so much a reflection of Espo's slowness
as it is of Cornoyer's speed, which was simply blinding. If
the two of them raced further, out on a great frozen lake,
it wouldn't be long before the Road Runner'd be just a dot
on the horizon.

"Skating at speed is just not easy for Esposito; and maybe
Bobby Clarke's in that category too: they have different
body types. They have to *work* to generate power. But
being awkward and slow doesn't mean that you're a terrible
skater," Sinden went on. "They learn how to protect the
puck as they come up the ice—the way a basketball guard
does when he dribbles the ball up the court. They compensate."

"What next?" I asked.

"Well, strength is certainly an important element in a
hockey player," Sinden said after a pause. "I keep thinking
of Bryan Trottier of the Islanders. Very strong on his skates.
He can take a tremendous bodycheck and not budge.
Gordie Howe, of course. Mark Messier of the Edmonton
Oilers. He's a kind of horse. Strength is important because
it tends to intimidate. When you get hit by a bodycheck by
any of the people I've named, it's bone-shattering. You
remember. You know when they're out there on the ice.
It's a force you feel as soon as the guy comes over the
boards."

I asked if strength wasn't something a player could build
up on his own—Nautilus machines and so forth.

"Of course," Sinden said. "But great skill is involved—
an ability to keep the weight perfectly distributed. These
people are seldom knocked off their skates whether giving
or receiving a check. You can't learn that in a weight
room."

"What about bodychecking?"

"A great asset—especially with the Boston Bruins who rely on it so much. Terry O'Reilly. A master at it. Johnny Bucyk. It's an art because you've got to ride the man off the puck and control it. If you miss the puck, both the puck and the man are gone. The other factor about good bodychecking, of course, is the intimidation. When these guys I've mentioned, or Mark Messier, or Denis Potvin are on the ice, they don't allow you to play with abandon."

"What else would be an important element?" I asked.

"I would certainly add checking," Sinden said.

"Bodychecking? I thought we'd just covered that."

"No. Checking is the art of getting the puck away from the other guy without riding him off it—like making a steal in basketball. Bobby Clarke of the Flyers would be an example of a great checker. Dogged. Keeps after you. A great ability to read a player and know what moves he is going to make with the puck. And courage too, because the great checker is always working away in tight quarters. He's not a big man, 175 maybe, 5'8". And then, once he had the puck, Clarke knew instantly what to do with it; he could make a play *off* a check—initiate an offense. That's rare. Think how many times you've seen a great check and then the puck given right back.

"Of course, I should add there have been some good players, important to the team, who couldn't do this, who couldn't check worth a damn. Pierre Larouche couldn't check his hat, as they say. You could avoid him all night long, like he was hiding out there. But he was a great scorer, and that more than compensated."

We got talking about shot making. Sinden decided that he would like to give his composite Gordie Howe's and Bobby Orr's. He mentioned Bobby Hull's, and in more contemporary times, Mike Bossy's of the New York Islanders. They all had what goaltenders often spoke woefully of—what is called a *heavy* shot: the puck seemed to take on dimensions of mass and density as it flew in on the nets. Gump Worsley described the phenomenon as being like a ten-pound boulder on the fly arriving at the goalmouth.

Accuracy and quickness were obviously characteristics enjoyed by the great shooter. *Release* was also an operative distinction, the ability to get the shot off with despatch and power usually while the player was moving in full stride.

"In hockey you can't pull up to take a shot," Sinden said, "like wheeling an artillery piece into position." The four players he had mentioned were wonderfully proficient at what he called "a snap"—a short slap shot in which the blade of the hockey stick only comes back about six or eight inches.

"What about a tactical sense?" I asked. "How important is that?"

Sinden winced and said, "You can have a player who skates badly, or who can't shoot, or who won't bodycheck, but up here if a player doesn't have a great tactical sense of what to do on the ice, that'll get him sent down to the minors quicker than anything . . . players who give the puck away or don't know what to do with it. It's better to have a player on the bench than out there making mistakes like that. I've always told my players if you don't know what to do with the puck, don't do anything with it. Get down on your knees and get it under you. You're better off with a face-off. Players who indiscriminately give up the puck, just turn it over to the other team, are doing the one thing coaches can't abide. It'll keep them out of the league.

"I think that tactically, Bobby Orr was just about the best there ever was. And now Wayne Gretzky. Gretzky sees

something that the rest of us don't. He gathers in information long before the rest of us do. He has that ability that
great pool players have—to make a play or a move that is
in preparation for something that he's going to do down the
line."

"And motivation?" I asked.

"Terry O'Reilly for motivation," Sinden said promptly.
I don't think there's ever been a player in the league to
compare with him in that department—Bobby Clarke of the
Flyers possibly. The remarkable fact about Terry is that he
played with such authority though he had limited ability.
He just oozed motivation and mental preparation. To watch
him on the ice was to want to emulate him. You couldn't
sit on the bench without being embarrassed if you couldn't
catch a sense of that force."

I asked Sinden if he didn't feel that kind of spirit was
endemic in other sports as well. "I don't think to the same
degree," he said. He went on: "Sports writers tell me
they're always impressed by the intensity that dominates
hockey players. The competitiveness. They're amazed by it.
Last year Hartford was out of the play-offs, nothing to gain
at all, and I think they won all their games but one.

"Mental attitude is a very important part of a hockey
player's equipment. What you hope is that it's consistent.
Orr was close to being a totally consistent player. Other
players, sometimes very good ones, have highs and lows.
Rick Middleton would be an example. Ken Hodge. A rol-
lercoaster. Obviously, the mental outlook must be a factor
in such cases, since you don't lose your skating ability. Who
knows what it is. If it's a bear market, perhaps they're
thinking about their stock portfolios. Goaltenders especially tend to have their highs and lows, but then perhaps
that's in the nature of that position."

"I suppose I ought to ask you about goaltenders."

"There are three qualities a goaltender must have," Sinden said. "He's got to have brains—a good, quick mind in order to read what's going on in front of him. To anticipate. Physical movement is not enough on its own . . . not quick enough . . . *can't* be that quick. So you have to be able to move toward the puck. Second of course, you have to possess the physical attributions—quick hands, good eyes, and strong legs. And finally you have to have courage."

"No flinching," I said. "No covering your eyes with your gloves."

"Exactly. And a good pair of pads," he went on with a grin. "Got to have those. What is interesting is that you had those qualifications—brains (you run some mind of literary magazine, don't you?), physical attributes—hands, eyes, legs, and so forth—and certainly you had courage. Or lunacy."

"And I had a pair of pads," I added.

"That's right. It's all relative."

I was telling my friend, Rick Smith, about Sinden's composite player. "It's interesting," he said. He paused a half second. "When you think about it, each of the last four decades has had its great superstars . . . Gordie Howe, then Bobby Hull, Bobby Orr, and now Wayne Gretzky. All played different positions, with each doing a completely different thing on the ice. Howe was mean, ruthless, graceful on his skates, yet like a mountain . . . you couldn't move him. Static, when it was important to him. Hull had the perfect hockey player's build, like he was sculpted, and he was fast, flying all over the rink, and he shot like a cannon: a blast! Then Orr came along. Leaner than Hull, and quick, he came from a different part of the rink, a defenseman, and he saw everything in front of him like a field general. A quarterback. And now Gretzky. Skinny. Frail-looking. Yet absolutely dominant in the offensive zone. When the puck is near him, he becomes a magician. All four of them completely different. All of them brilliant and dominant forces." He laughed. "You don't need a composite with those guys around." He shook his head. "You had to feel privileged just being on the ice with any one of them."

14

THERE were vast changes. Trades. Retirements. Rick Smith retired and began studying computer science. Brad Park went to the Detroit Red Wings, Wayne Cashman retired. John Wensink, the enforcer, went to the New Jersey Devils, and then himself retired. Cheevers too, in 1985, was fired and replaced by Harry Sinden. The bumblebee black and gold, as I watched them from my seat, were no longer the faces and skating styles I had come to know, but rather symbols of the organization I was rooting for.

For me there were still blanks to be filled. I called up Phil Esposito, who heads the Phil Esposito Foundation set up to promulgate the cause and well-being of old-timers, to ask if they had Gilles Gratton's address in their files. I still hoped to get the story from the former Ranger goaltender on how he had streaked the Maple Leaf Gardens.

"You won't find him," Esposito said. "He was the craziest player we ever had. Spaced out. One night, he wouldn't play because the moon was in the wrong part of the sky. He didn't want to come to the Garden. He thought he might look up on the way and see it, which was apparently the worst thing that could happen, and very bad luck. They asked me to talk to him. I told him he could make the Garden safely by concentrating on his feet, watching when

he put one in front of the other. 'Just keep your head down,
Gilles, and you'll make it.' He did, too."

"What about streaking the Gardens?" I asked.

"I was there! I saw him. He came sailing out on the ice
during practice wearing his skates, socks, his goaltender's
mask, and wearing a jock strap. Nothing else! Strangest
thing to see you ever saw! He must have been getting ready
to do it in public, because in the last game of the season in
the Garden, Gratton told us he was going to start a strip
right there in the goal during the last period. He was finishing with hockey. His last year. It seemed just the right kind
of gesture, at least from Gilles. He promised! He was going
to start the strip just before the end of the game. Everyone
knew about it, including John Ferguson, the Rangers coach
at the time. In the locker room between periods we'd look
over and see Fergy trying to talk him out of it. Gratton
would always nod his head and promise, but then when
he'd walk by us, he'd say 'Watch! Watch!'

"We wanted him to. So did he, I think. He kept saying
'Watch! Watch!'

"At the end of the third period we kept looking down
toward him in our goal. We'd clap our gloves together and
bang our sticks like it looked we were applauding him for
a great game. But what we were really doing, of course, was
urging him on. He never did it. He let us down something
terrible. It would have been quite a sight to look down and
see your goaltender standing there buck-ass with a big pile
of gear next to him. He could have done it, too. I mean who
was going to come out on the ice and stop him? The Garden
attendants?" Esposito laughed. "They would have had to
send the Zamboni after him."

I said that if it had ever crossed *my* mind to do such a
thing—on a huge dare, say—I was so inept with all that
goaltending gear that to get it off before the game ended

I'd have had to start plucking away at my uniform after only a minute or so into the period.

I asked, "Espo, is it true you fell on a rose petal in Moscow?"

"Did I ever! Flat out on the ice! It was from the bouquet they gave me. I must have squeezed a petal loose in my nervousness. Down I went. The next night I skated out and held onto the boards during the pregame ceremonies. I don't know what the Russians made of it, but of course everyone in Canada, watching on television, caught on to what I was doing, and why. I blew Comrade Brezhnev a kiss, too. Did I tell you that?"

"No, but it doesn't surprise me. Nothing I hear from hockey players surprises me any more."

I MET Bobby Orr. We did a television show together in which I interviewed him on skates in a rink in San Diego; I got in the goal at one point and he scored on me. The show was part of a series. Earlier that year I had been scored on by Pelé, the great soccer star, so for a time I went around remarking that in one year I had been scored on by both Pelé and Bobby Orr.

Orr loved to tell anecdotes.

He told me about an old-timer now a coach, he thought, at Portland named Tommy McVee, who had lost all his teeth in the hockey wars and who took advantage of their lack by perfecting a trick in which he would catch a puck in his glove up near his face, and then somehow get it into his mouth. "It was gone!" From there he could make it emerge from his toothless gums as if the shot had gone into his head and he was spitting it out. It was a very funny sight, Orr said, and the memory of the puck appearing, the player's eyes popping as his tongue pushed it out, would get

Orr laughing so hard he could hardly describe the scene.

Orr laughs very easily. One had the sense that just about anything would affect him as comical—eye-squeezing laughter. One story he could barely tell because of its comic aspects was the time they stole Esposito out of the Massachusetts General Hospital and into the Branding Iron. It took a while for Orr to recount this, he got laughing so hard.

I got him talking about Wayne Gretzky. "Wait'll you watch him. He can see the whole ice surface. He doesn't hesitate. He's five, ten seconds ahead of everyone else. They say his only flaw is defense . . . but since he has the puck all the time it's difficult to imagine that as a flaw. He's a helluva kid, too. The money hasn't spoiled him in the slightest."

I asked Bobby what the Bruins had done to get *him* into their organization.

"They agreed to stucco my parents' house. Nineteen sixty-six. I was eighteen. I got a check for twelve hundred dollars and ten dollars a week for spending money."

I remember them saying around the table at the Peter Pan that scouts who saw him early felt that Orr could have played with the Bruins when he was twelve.

He was mentioning that now his knees were so bad that he had to turn down an easy game of hackers' tennis. "My legs couldn't handle it." But he wanted to assure me that it had been worth it. "I would not have wanted to go through life wondering if I could have done it."

PHIL ESPOSITO was telling me about the signing procedures.

"I've always wondered," I had asked. "How do you get signed up at the age of twelve or thirteen?"

"What happened was that the scouts or the managers would turn up in Sault Ste. Marie, or some other small town, and they'd offer the parents five hundred or maybe a thousand dollars if the kid was something really special. The forms they had in their suitcases were called the 'C' forms, and that meant, if your parents signed it, that you were tied up for life with one of the six teams in the league. If my brother or I ever turned pro we *had* to play for the Chicago Black Hwks."

"Did the parents sit around to see if anyone else turned up with a higher bid?"

"Well, that's what happened with Bobby Hull," Esposito said. "Bob Wilson, who was the chief scout of the Black Hawks got to Point Ann, Ontario, about an hour in front of the chief scout of the Red Wings."

"Why did the parents sign so quickly?"

Esposito said, "Well, in those days, in some little town, when you were offered a thousand dollars on the *possibilty* that a twelve-year-old kid was going to make it in professionals—only a handful of teams, remember—they'd say to themselves at the kitchen table, 'Well, he's never gonna make hockey anyway,' and they'd sign the 'C' paper."

"It must be a heady experience for a twelve year old to be signed to a professional organization."

"Oh yes. I liked the Black Hawks uniform. To this day their uniforms and the Bruins' are the best. Beautiful."

"And you had your younger brother, Tony, to practice your shot against."

"That's right. He became a goaltender because of me. I was older and authoritative enough. I got him to stand in front of makeshift nets in the back of the yard so I could fire pucks at him. He had no choice. And then in the summertime we'd go down in the basement and play knee hockey —batting my father's rolled socks around with our hands, maybe four or five kids from the neighborhood down there with us. We'd stick him in the goal. Of course, it's one thing to be hit with a rolled-up sock and quite another when it's a puck."

"It must have been an odd sensation playing against him once you both got to the NHL."

He grinned. "I have always had great luck playing against my brother because down in the basement and out in the backyard I got to know all his moves. When we played against each other, my mom couldn't take it. She always saw Tony as the last line of defense and when he was scored on, he looked so dejected, so depressed, she couldn't bear to watch. My dad . . . he laughs with the winner and cries with the loser and everything is O.K. Tony's first game in the NHL was in the Boston Garden. He had just been called up and was playing for Montreal then. The score ended up in a 2–2 tie. His wife—she was in Houston at the time—called me up because she hadn't heard from Tony.

"She asked, 'What happened. I haven't heard . . .'

"I said, 'He played terrific. He really did. It was a 2–2.'

"So she said, 'Thank you, oh boy, thank you, Lord,' and so forth, and then she asked, 'Did you score on him?'

"I said, 'Yeah, I got one.'

"She asked, 'Who got the other one?'

"I said, 'I got the other one, too.'

"At that she called me a few names and hung up the phone."

THE phone rang one afternoon and it was Gilles Gratton. He had heard I was trying to find him. First he told me he was in town drumming up interest for a meditiation organization. The Spiritual Master, who was an Indian woman, was arriving in a few days time to conduct a three-week seminar. That was his *news*. What did I want from him?

I said I was hoping to find out something about his former lives.

"What have you heard?"

"Well, I heard you were a soldier who had been stabbed . . ."

"That's not accurate. I was a Spanish landowner, very large property holder. Then at some point in the eighteenth century I was a Spanish priest."

"Not an archduke. I'd heard . . ."

"Not at all. In the nineteenth century I was a British surgeon living in Germany and doing research on the heart and lungs."

"I see. What about streaking the Maple Leaf Gardens?? Is that true?"

"That was terribly overblown," Gratton said. "It wasn't the Gardens to begin with. It was a little practice rink close by. I came out naked after practice and skated around. I did that a *lot*—to tell you the truth—it *felt* good. But this one time there happened to be a reporter sitting in there and he saw me come sailing out. Must have surprised him. He wrote about it and it all got blown out of proportion."

"What did you like about it?"

"Well, hockey is boring, which is why I quit it, and skating around like that is *not* boring."

"It wasn't the Gardens?"

"Oh hell, you'd have to be *nuts* to skate around naked in the Maple Leaf Gardens."

E D D I E   S H O R E died. I thought about going up to Springfield for the funeral, but it would have seemed odd to be attending services for a gentleman I had never met. Shortly after leaving the Bruins I had tried to see him. The stories Don Cherry had told me about him were hard to forget. I managed to reach his nephew, Jack Butterfield, the president of the American Hockey League, who lives in Springfield. He gave me his uncle's telephone number. Shore answered. I introduced myself and said I hoped to come to Springifled to see him . . . perhaps talk about the old times . . . go to a game with him. . . .

"You a writer?"

I said I was.

"No!" he said, and the receiver went into its cradle with quite a crack.

Butterfield was not surprised. He said that Shore very rarely appeared in public; he was vain, sometimes in a nursing home, and he wanted people to remember him as he was.

"What did he do after hockey?" I asked.

"He played golf. With exactly the same intensity he gave to hockey. He got down to a three handicap before he had his heart troubles. He had a golf net out in his backyard with a canvas backing, and overhead lights so he could go out there at night and hit a bag of balls. Drove the neighbors just crazy. The golf ball'd hit that canvas backstop and make a sound like a gunshot. He had tremendous power. I once saw him hit a golf ball 325 yards. In the wintertime he had the same sort of net set up inside in one of the spare rooms; on the coldest nights, three feet of snow outside, the neighbors could hear that awful crack and see his shadow against the window shade."

"What was he like on the golf course?" I asked.

"About what you'd expect," Butterfield said. "Tempestuous. He'd think nothing of hurling a golf club across a fairway. Or walking out in the middle of a tournament."

"Did he have any golfing advice?"

"Oh yes. Wouldn't have been like him not to. You had to sit back, kind of, bending your knees when you addressed the ball . . . "

I was tempted to ask—remembering what Don Cherry had told me—if the stance was at all like going to the bathroom in the woods.

" . . . bend your knees," Butterfield was saying. "That was a *big* thing with him. No matter what you did, you had to bend your knees."

When we got off golf and began chatting about Eddie Shore and hockey, Butterfield felt that for all his antediluvian methods of communication he was miles ahead of his time. "He just wasn't very good at explaining things."

"So I understand," I said.

"When the Russian hockey teams turned up here with those great teams, we all saw what Shore wanted of his players years before. It was like they had sent spies to watch. 'Never stand still'—that was how he put it. He had excellent theories, but he could not take the time to explain them. You had to accept what he said or you were stupid. There were a few who benefitted. Parker MacDonald came down to Springfield from the Detroit Red Wings. When he arrived in camp, Shore said, 'I'm going to teach you *one* thing. If you do that, you'll score 40 goals a season.'

" 'What's that?'

" 'When you come into the net to take your shot, put your skates *down* and stop. Most guys sail around the ice, go around behind the net, after they've taken their shot. Stop when you shoot, and, mister, you'll get a lot of rebounds.' MacDonald followed his advice and became a great scorer."

"He called everyone 'mister,' didn't he?"

"Either 'mister' or 'young man.' I was his nephew, knew him every day for over thirty years, and I don't think I once heard him call me 'Jack.' It's been said before, but when they built him, they threw the mold away."

He was buried in the Hillcrest Park Cemetery in Springfield. Afterwards the mourners gathered at the Storroton
Tavern to reminisce. Many of them were old-timers:
Gordie Howe, Emile Francis, Tom Johnson from the
Bruins, King Clancy, Pat Egan. The Storroton was where
Shore would go to eat after a game—usually swordfish, and
inevitably carrots and beets. He had a glass of brandy.
Sometimes he went out to thank the chef. Everyone in the
kitchen jumped when he appeared through the swinging
doors. The old-timers closed up the Storroton. They sat
swapping stories and would have stayed until the dawn if
it were not for the licensing laws.

W H E N I heard about Shore's death I telephoned Don
Cherry. He had told me such extraordinary stories about
him that I thought he would have an interesting comment
or two. Or maybe another story. He had left coaching
completely and was now the host of a television program
out of Toronto. From time to time, I was told, his pit terrier,
Blue, appeared on the show with him, sitting in her own
chair, nodding slightly.

We talked about Blue for a while, which was always the
form after being out of touch for a while. Then I mentioned
Shore. His mood changed abruptly. "They called him a
great man. Let them. For me," he said, "there was no
sorrow whatsoever. I'd be a hypocrite if I said anything else.
He caused me, my family, such terrible times. He made
hockey a horror."

I changed the subject. I wondered if hockey had been
easy to leave.

Cherry was just as vehement on *that* subject. "Hockey is
the only sport in the world where if you're through, that's
it: you're treated like a leper. You'll never see an older
player go down to the dressing room after a game. He's

scared of being classified as a 'floater.' Once you've gone, you're gone."

I asked if there was any club in the league which looked after its old-timers.

Cherry answered: "The only club which has any concern about this is, as you might expect, Montreal. The Canadiens. In the Forum they have a room set aside for their old-timers. It's down the corridor; the old players can go in there with their wives and sit around. Yes," he said, "they have cookies for them."

I SPOKE to John Wensink on the phone. I had always remembered what he had said so simply about Don Cherry's support of him. "Don Cherry est mon père." He was now in the construction business in St. Louis. I could hear his children shouting gaily in the background. We talked about his doll houses. He said his kids had broken a bedroom door in one of them. But after all, that was what they were for, wasn't it? To play with? I mentioned how lucky it was that he was in the construction business; a broken door in a doll house was probably a pretty simple matter for him.

"Was being out of hockey hard?" I asked. It had struck me that in his case—perhaps unlike Cherry's—it wouldn't be at all difficult to step down from such a violent world of retribution and thugee behavior; I said as much.

Wensink said, "Oh no, that was all left on the ice, the bad feelings, and it was a great shock to leave hockey and very hard. It had been the best of times. But what happens," he explained, "is that you see your teammates every day, and then when it's over, it's over. You never see them again. You wonder why so-and-so who was your friend, and you roomed with him on the road trips, wouldn't give a call when he comes through town. You could sit around and tell

stories. Have a beer. He could come to your house and see
your children. Maybe look at the doll houses. But they
don't call. They never call. You wonder. You wonder.
After you leave, there is no contact with anyone. It hurts.
It makes you feel like you're a gust in the wind."

"John, what do you remember about the fight in Philly
—the one I missed."

"I'm never going to forget it," he assured me. "I was a
little worried, let me tell you. You'll remember a lot of us
were having our skates sharpened from scuffling around on
the concrete of the corridors. On the ice we were outnumbered. When I came down the ramp to the ice there were
three of them waiting for me—Harry Bennett, Hound Dog
Kelly, and Bob Dailey. We went down in a big pile out on
the ice. Nobody threw a punch. I still don't know why. I
knew why I didn't: they could have killed me. Nobody said
anything. I don't even remember hearing the crowd although they were going crazy watching what was going on.
Just the four of us breathing in that big pile."

I was reminded of how much it resembled O'Reilly's
experience. I asked if he missed the fighting. He laughed.
He told me about his final experience as an enforcer. He
had finished his career playing in Holland. His forebears
came from there to Ontario, so it was appropriate enough.
He played for the Nijmegen Vissors, the name of a local
furniture company which sponsored the team.

"We were playing the Einhoven Phillips. I was sitting on
the bench with a pulled groin. It was the end of the season.
We went behind in this game 3-0 . . . a Canadian player
named Michel Garleone scoring all the goals—a hat-trick
against us. Well, after a while the coach looked over at me
and he said, 'John, would you like one more shift.' I knew
what he was talking about. I said, 'Sure, I'd love to go.' So
I went out and broke my thumb on Michel Garleone. Both
of us were thrown out of the game."

"What was the final score?" I could not resist asking.

"We won 4–3." Wensink could barely contain himself. "It worked."

"John, what sort of effect would this kind of thing have on Wayne Gretzky?"

"I wouldn't think twice about running him. I'm amazed he hasn't been taken out of the play more often. Amazed! He's been great for hockey, but that's no reason he shouldn't be thumped. They do that from kids up; it was part of the game. It makes sense tactically. I go out and thump Gretzky. He's going to stand up for himself. So that's two minutes for him in the penalty box, and five minutes for me. Right there, that's better for my team than it was with him on the ice. Probably, at the same time, someone on the Oilers will jump in to help him, which invokes the third-man rule and that guy goes off with a ten-minute misconduct. Now we get a man advantage for a while. It makes sense, but these days the teams don't have so many guys who will go out and thump. The values have changed. A lot of guys were put out of work."

D A V E "The Hammer" Schultz and Wensink never fought—very likely, at least these days, to the relief of both. When I chatted with Schultz, he too talked about the curious code that the enforcers went by—that what they were to do on the ice was always suggested by inference and innuendo. They always knew their function and their place. If Schultz happened to score a goal or two, his coach, Shero, would say, "Well, I guess I'd better get myself another tough guy."

"Is it easy, afterwards, to meet someone you've had a fight with?"

"I've never had a fight off the ice if that's what you mean."

"Two different personalities?"

"Yup." He says "yup" like a farmer.

"I meant if you ran into someone at a banquet . . ."

"Oh, we'd probably laugh about it. I'd say, ''I won that one.' Not long ago I ran into Kurt Walker of the Maple Leafs. He had been sent into a game to take care of me. I punched him and he went down in a heap. Then he got up and spat at me . . . for which they gave him a ten-minute misconduct. When we met some time ago, we had a nice chat, not about the fight, but life, and how he had been getting along. Actually, you find that you have an easier time talking to guys like that. You have more in common. It's much easier than talking to a real good hockey player."

I asked him about his model boats.

"And airplanes."

"I didn't know about the airplanes."

"Yup. But I haven't had much time for them any more. The great pleasure was in making them, really. Woodwork. I do a lot of that. I like putting things together. I can spend ten hours straight working on a jigsaw puzzle."

Once again, I thought what a remarkable contrast: someone spending all those hours putting an intricate thing together who that evening would go out and live up to his sobriquet—"The Hammer."

"Did you know that John Wensink makes doll houses?"

"No kidding," the Hammer said. "Think of that."

PERHAPS the busiest man on the ice the night I was sipping a cool beer in the Ovation Room in the Spectrum was the referee, Wally Harris. Not long ago, I had occasion to ask him if he remembered the fracas.

"Oh yes," he said. "The fighting was back in the runways under the stands."

I asked if what had gone on back there was actually under his jurisdiction. After all, it had all taken place quite a distance from the rink.

"Oh yes," Harris said. "Anything that bears on the game itself is our responsibility. The guys who really saved that situation were Keith Allen and Harry Sinden, the general managers of the clubs. It could have been very bad if it weren't for the two of them cooling things down and trying to keep players out of the corridors."

I asked, "What sort of thing do you say to break up a fight?"

"If you'll excuse my language, it's just a lot of bullshit. Anything that comes to mind often works. You tell them to cool it. You might say, 'Christ, you couldn't beat up your wife. Get out of there before you get killed.' It always helps to have a kind of rapport with the players themselves. That's why older officials often have an easier time bringing things under control. They know the guys, and what might cool them down. Sometimes even a *look* will do it."

"Why do you let the fights go on for as long as they do?"

"Well, if it's a brawl, it pretty much cools down by itself. There's not much you can do. You *hope* it cools down before someone gets hurt—and that's a terrible possibility when twenty guys are rolling around with skate edges like razors. But nothing much can happen when two guys are squaring off against each other. They haven't got good balance to begin with. Someone's going to go down fairly quickly. Then you step in. But you've got to let them get it out of their systems. If you interfere too early, they haven't let the steam out. They'll fight again."

I asked Harris how he had been able to keep track of all the infractions that night in Philadelphia. Was he jotting things down in a notebook?

"Some officials have little notepads. I've never used

one," Harris said, "You train yourself to memorize . . . to start picking numbers in a hurry and remembering them when you go over to the officials' table. When you have a big brawl, forty people out there dancing, you've got to be selective, so that you've got enough people left on the ice to continue the game. So you pick the instigators, which is usually easy: you know who they are to begin with. The ones I don't like are the sneaky ones who start something, and they're not around when you look. The true enforcers dish it out right in front of you. They play the same way in every rink. The sneaky ones are a pain in the ass."

"Did you ever get the sense it could get completely out of hand . . . ?"

"Oh no," Harris said. "I rather enjoyed the one in Philly. The only thing I didn't like was knowing I'd have to sit down and write a long report. Incidentally, where were you?" he asked.

"I was hoping you wouldn't bring it up," I said. "I was having a beer in the Ovation Room. I didn't know the brawl was going on. It's the greatest gaffe of my journalistic career. I wanted to be there. I wanted to be able to tell Seaweed Pettie, who was my roommate in training camp, and a brawling goalie himself, what it was like. I wanted to come down the runway out onto the ice . . ."

Harris said, "You and I could have started figure skating at center ice. That might have stopped everything. Or you could have skated out and tried to hide behind me. I wouldn't have known *what* to do."

A L A S , Seaweed did not make it in the majors. The report I had was that while he was wondrously quick and adept at the stick handling and leg saves he was weak in the catching and control aspects of goaltending. He stayed with the Rochester Americans for a while and then quit to get married and start life first as an auto salesman, and then working in a factory. I dropped in to see him at his home in Rochester. He had lost none of his enthusiasm and intensity. The image crossed my mind of what a hectic time his potential customers must go through in the showroom.

Now, he said, he was working on an assembly line, fixing machines. "Guess what," he told me. "I took a test. They told me I had no reflexes, hardly any hand-to-eye coordination, and my depth perception was way off. Physically they didn't feel I was up to working on the assembly line. That's why I'm fixing machines."

"Did you tell them that you played goal for the Bruins?"

"They would have laughed in my face," Seaweed said. "They would have sent me down to take a psychiatrist's examination."

We reminisced about my stay with the Bruins. I said, "Every once in a while, Seaweed, I'm reminded of all of you, and that good experience, by the oddest thing. Opening a closet, to get a suit out, I occasionally get just the faintest whiff of that odor I remember about training camp —that combination of funk and old sweat that seemes to drift off my pads. . . ."

Seaweed was laughing.

"Oh, you fell for it." He could barely contain himself. "That wasn't funk," he said. "Or old sweat. That was some kind of jelly that came off a bottle Wayne Cashman bought in a novelty shop. I think it was called U-STINK, something like that. 'Essence of Egg.' We smeared it on your clothes when you were out on the ice."

He was almost out of control. I was aghast. I said: "You know what? I thought it was a good honest smell—like what drifts off a farmer's coveralls. I kept hoping someone on a bus would lean over and ask, 'You've played a lot of goal, right?' "

Seaweed was slapping his knees.

I went on. "The number of people I must have offended, or at the very least startled with that smell. My God, Seaweed, I went to New York a couple of times. My family never said anything."

"They were being polite," he said. "God, we could tell when you were coming around a corner in the motel."

"No!"

"That's right. 'Here he comes!' You remember the night we went to see *Star Wars* and the people around us were gasping?"

I could not remember but I cringed to think of it.

When Seaweed finally calmed down, he began chatting about Wayne Gretzky, the great Edmonton Oiler star. Gretzky seemed to come into the conversation with just about all the Bruins I talked to. Seaweed talked about him with the enthusiasm and awe that made me think of the evenings in the taverns of Fitchburg reminiscing about Bobby Orr.

"Why can't they intimidate him?" I asked. "He only weighs, what? 170 pounds. John Wensink was saying that he was surprised he hadn't been pushed around a bit."

"He's so fluid," Seaweed said. "He'd slide through mesh. All arms and legs. Nothing to hit. Quick he sees you coming. And then he's got some protection—Dave Semenko, big guy who goes out, cruising around, looking out for him."

Seaweed told me about a shot he had heard Gretzky had made from behind the opposition's net. He had been trying to pass it out to a teammate, the goaltender scurrying back and forth from one net post to the other, sneaking quick looks back to see at which angle the puck would come out, and suddenly Gretzky flipped the puck over on edge so he could chip it over the net. It hit the goalie in the back of his helmet, rolled down the numbers of his jersey and into the net.

"Come on," I said. "Do you mean he did that on purpose?"

"That's what they say," Seaweed said. "I'd believe just about anything about that guy."

I could hear his daughter's small voice calling for him from another room. Seaweed said he had to go to her. "My daughter wants to iron," he explained.

N O T long after seeing Seaweed Pettie in Rochester, by coincidence I happened to be asked to Edmonton. I was asked to give a speech to a Junior Achievement organization sponsored in part by the Edmonton Oilers hockey club. Wouldn't it be appropriate, the organizers suggested, if I went out on the ice during the Oilers' morning scrimmages so I could tell the kids who were being honored that night what it was like to be in the goal against Wayne Gretzky. At first, I demurred. I had done it all before. I had struggled with Dornhoefer in the crease. I had been scored on by Bobby Orr.

But there was always that nagging suspicion that if I did not take them up on their offer, I would ultimately regret it: "You mean you had a chance to be on the ice with *Gretzky*—the greatest player who ever lived—and you turned it down?"

I remembered what Rick Smith had said—what a privilege it had been for him to be on the ice with the four great hockey players of his generation: Howe, Hull, Orr, and Gretzky.

Certainly what they all said about him seemed to check out. With its point system hockey has an accurate method of measuring the caliber of its stars. Not only does the scorer get a point for his goal, but an assist counts for a point as well. Usually the last two players who touch the puck on its way to the scorer get accredited. One hundred points in a season was considered an astonishing mark to achieve. Bobby Orr did it first, then Phil Esposito. They did it a couple of times, and were joined by a few more—Guy Lafleur and Marcel Dionne of the Canadiens, Mike Bossy and Bryan Trottier of the Islanders. But Gretzky, year after year, has been finishing 50–60 points ahead of his nearest competition which means, in theory at least, that he is a third better than anyone else in the league. It was as if in baseball a hitter consistently had a batting average well over .400.

Gretzky's somewhat detached observation about his own skills was that they were attributable to a kind of symbiotic relationship with the puck itself. His father had always believed that intuitive behavior could be taught. His son, who was started off at hockey at the age of two, had developed an understanding of the game equivalent to the way geniuses take to a musical instrument, or chess.

So I accepted the invitation of the Junior Achievement organization. It seemed absurd not to. I found my goaltender's skates in a bag in the back of a closet, the black pocked leather shiny and unused-looking. I expected to find the mask with the blue eye painted on the face; no sign of it. I have no idea what happened to it—perhaps it has ended up in good hands, at this very moment with eyes behind it peering out at Peewee League action somewhere. I told my family I was going up to Edmonton. My mother discovered my plans. She wanted to know why I couldn't do it all by phone. She is a great believer in modern communications systems.

15

THE first view of Edmonton, at least coming in from the airport, is astonishing. One drives past miles of three- and four-story frame buildings, a little higher and fancier as one goes, until finally the visitor assumes there'll be more of the same, and that's Edmonton. But then one goes over the rise of a hill and the modern skyscraper city rises out of the deep valley like a mirage. It reminded me of Pittsburgh —coming through the tunnel on the airport side of the Monongaheela and the sudden visual shock of seeing the cluttered towers of the Golden Triangle across the river.

My hosts dropped me off at the arena. Someone had written off to one side of the players' entrance with a graffiti pen: "Gretzky's House."

Ted Green, one of the assistant coaches, took me in hand. We chatted first about the Bruins, a link, Green having played with them, first as an enforcer—what he himself called being an "aggressive player"—until a terrible injury from a hockey-stick fracas in an exhibition against the St. Louis Blues in 1969 left him with a plate in his head. Rick Smith had told me about the incident. He had been on hand when it occurred—Green smashed by a hockey stick wielded by Wayne Maki in front of the St. Louis net.

"Before that instant," Rick had said, "Ted was just plain *mean*—terrified the daylights out of me. On the ice people

were scared to go near him. 'Terrible Ted,' he was called.
When he was injured, I thought his face was simply caved
in by Maki's stick. Paralyzed on one side. Speech gone. But
what then happened was that he came back after a long
period of recuperation and readjusted the style of his game
—which in fact had been built mostly on instilling fear—to
relying on athletic skills. It was an incredible achievement.
Dave Schultz—your friend, The Hammer—tried to do the
same thing, but it didn't work. Green had always been a
team leader—Orr under his wing, and Esposito, and Eddie
Johnston, the goaltender, and he had a lot to do with the
team becoming the great force it was through the seventies.
It's a remarkable story, and I'd guess Green has had much
the same influence on Edmonton, which in thirteen months
went from mediocre to a championship team—two Stanley
Cups so far. Of course, they had Gretzky . . . but you have
to put a team around someone like that."

Green himself was less emphatic about the difference in
his styles before and after the accident, though he agreed
he was somewhat "more tentative" on his return. No wonder! His injuries not only paralyzed his left side, but his
recovery was fraught with complications, including convul-
sions from the drugs prescribed to him. His head hummed.
He would answer phones that had never rung. His left was
his natural side, which meant that he not only had to learn
to write with the other hand, but also shift the stick around
to play hockey right-handed. He still has no feeling in his
left hand. He says that when he's tired, a little hesitancy
develops in his speech.

I asked if he had ever thought of giving up the game
during his recuperation. He said that he probably should
have—the doctors urged it—but that the thought truly had
not entered his mind.

He showed me around the Edmonton clubhouse. We

stopped by the big curved screens of the video equipment.
Green said that it had become an essential part of hockey
coaching. "I have a lot of respect from the past to the
present, but the players now are bigger, better, stronger—
we're looking at a prospect for the Oilers who is 6'5", 220
pounds, and for his all-around ability, not necessarily his
aggressiveness—and the *coaching* is better. The game is so
much more sophisticated. Stanley Cups are won because of
this kind of material."

He pointed at the screen. "During the play-offs we prepare footage up to 45 minutes in length which we show to
the team the day before the series. We condense that, and
they see it on the day of the game after the pregame skate.
There's a very close analysis of what they see on the film.
It's not puck-in-the-corner anymore. Any team which doesn't use video and film would *have* to fall behind the
times."

I said that when I was there at Boston Don Cherry also
used the video machine, but only to show the various tri-
umphs of the prior game, never the mistakes. The team
would lose 8–1 and he'd show the one goal scored, often
set to music. Invariably, he showed the fights, these also set
to the wild strains of rock and roll. The players loved it. The
video was on hand as a kind of morale booster.

Green nodded and mentioned that Gretzky used the
video in just such a way. "He loves to watch the good
things. We get the footage together for him. He's been
having trouble scoring on breakaways. He sits in here and
analyzes what he does when he *succeeds*. It's something I
learned a lot about while recovering from my head injuries
—psychokinetics. Golfers perhaps use it more than anyone
—seeing in their mind's eye what they *should* do."

I asked Green what he thought Gretzky's greatest talent
was.

He added one I had not heard. "To me, it's his ability
to move laterally," Green said. "No one has ever done it
as well. Great running backs in football have that gift.
Gretzky can do it on ice, and at full speed. It's a gift which
allows him to dominate the game when he's out there."

Players had begun to drift into the clubhouse. I did not
recognize Gretzky among them. It was unsettling being there. Ted Green showed me to a locker stall and then
went off to attend to his coaching functions. The goaltending equipment lay in a substantial heap in front of
me.

Unlike the lepers' room at Fitchburg where I had settled
in after a while, and the faces were recognizable and
friendly, and I was part of the chatter and the ambiance,
here everything was foreign. A few of the Oilers who knew
I was going to be practicing with them that morning smiled,
and came over and introduced themselves. That made it
better. Still no sign of Gretzky. Indeed, there was some
question whether he would be practicing that morning. I
would go out anyway—nothing uninteresting about being on the ice with Kurri, Anderson, Semenko, and the
others. . . .

I took almost an hour to get the equipment on. I had
forgotten the procedures. I got the order wrong. I would
groan, strip down, and start again. The Oilers locker room
pulsed with the sound of a portable stereo set up on the
Ping-Pong table in the center of the room on which Gretzky
plays to relax before a game.

Ted Green reappeared and asked how I was getting
along.

"I don't feel very agile," I said.

Ted said, "You put on years when you put on a goaltender's equipment. A twenty-year old kid is suddenly in
middle age when he's got that stuff on."

"Well, if that's the proper progression," I said, "you're looking at an octogenarian!"

M Y entrance and progress on the ice were even more stately and ponderous than it had been in my Bruins days. Getting settled properly between the posts made me think of the docking of an ocean liner, lacking only the blasts from the horn and the creaking of the piles as the vast weight of the ship leaned against them. I jockeyed slowly in and turned around. I looked out at the long stretch of ice.

Then suddenly I saw Gretzky. He was on the ice, standing over by the boards talking to someone—a business manager perhaps, because I saw him sign a paper or an autograph. My first impression was that he looked nothing like a hockey player, or even an athlete. He reminded me of a high school band musician—perhaps a flute player. Nor, when he moved away from the boards, was he an intimidating figure on the ice—nothing at all awesome about him as I had been told was the immediate reaction on seeing the great slope of Gordie Howe's shoulders or the bullish conformities of Bobby Hull, or Bobby Orr beginning one of his rushes down the ice—characteristics which instantly suggested that something was in the building to be reckoned with.

But then, looking up from the goal mouth I saw him hunting now, wheeling out there around the vicinity of the blue line, rather like a hawk circling low over a hedgerow. It occurred to me later that it was not an inaccurate metaphor since it *was* rather like spotting a rare accipter, as in "My God, it's a Gretzky!" the way a birdwatcher might whisper, "Oh look, there's a Cooper's hawk over there."

He was not wearing his helmet (none of the Oilers were during the drills) so he was instantly recognizable, the boy-

ish face with the thin pronounced nose, and a curiously
smug smile underneath, the teeth shining in it when he
grinned, and a graceful, swooping style that seemed to
materialize him abruptly *here* and *there* on the ice. I could
see what Ted Green meant when he was talking about
Gretzky's great lateral movement. I don't know whether he
smiles all the time during practices, undoubtedly not, but
he wore one that morning, perhaps for my benefit, possibly
because of my gangling, hopeless demeanor in the goal.

They let me into the practice on occasion. I kept looking
for Gretzky. Once, he banked a shot in off my skate even
though there was barely enough room between the post
and the blade of my skate for the puck to slide through. He
did the same thing off my pads—little delicate flip shots,
calculated ricochets, the sort of thing more associated with
billiard tables.

During a break I went over and stood with him over by
the boards. I asked him about the shot Seaweed had described—the one flipped over the back of the cage which
had hit the goaltender in the back of the helmet and trickled
down his back into the goal. Oh yes, that was true, Gretzky
said. It happened in a game against St. Louis.

"Was it calculated?" I asked.

"It just seemed like the right shot to try."

He seemed almost embarrassed as he said this, though it
was also a divulgence he was delighted to make. He reminded me of a kid who has sneaked in and caught a huge
trout out of a posted pond and can't resist talking about it.

After practice, everyone milled around the rink, just as
they had at Boston—horsing about, wrestling, wind sprint
racing, practicing their shots. I saw a shot taken that I had
never seen before—what players called a "kick shot." It is
illegal, apparently. Don Jackson stood out by the center line
and called down to me (I was taking a turn in the goal) to be

on the lookout. He had a puck set down off to one side, the blade of his stick just behind it; with the stick held diagonally across his body, Jackson then strode forward and with a kicking motion he brought the stick sharply back across the shin of the kicking leg. The leverlike combination of the arm and leg motion snaps the hockey stick forward at a terrific clip (from close to it must twang like a bow) and the puck rose off the ice and came toward me on a direct line over half the length of the rink" and passed my head by two or three feet, with never a hint of dropping a millimeter or so as it came. A "rope" as they say in golf, or a "snake." It hit the glass behind me with an alarming crack. My jaw went agape inside my mask. It was as if another projectile, a new weapon, had been introduced into the game. Jackson came skating down. He saw how impressed I was. "Quite something, eh?" He said that he could stand on one blue line and with the "kick shot" drive the puck down the length of the ice, over the other blue line, and into the stands on a line. "It'll practically go through a seat," he said.

A T T H E end of the scrimmages (the banquet people thought it would provide material for my remarks that evening) Gretzky agreed to take a penalty shot. In fact, he took three. The Oilers stood along the boards to watch. Gretzky got a lot of joshing because, as Ted Green had told me, he was having trouble scoring on his one-on-one situations— breakaways and penalty shots.

Waiting at the mouth of the nets, I decided to do what had worked successfully against Reggie Leach of the Flyers —to emerge from the nets quickly and fling myself sideways to the ice (the antique-sofa-collapse maneuver) and hope that Gretzky would take his shot from out there and not keep the puck on his stick to come around my sliding bulk.

He picked up a puck from a cluster lying past the blue line and started his move. I sashayed out. To my astonishment he was past me before I could even initiate my collapse. It was as if we had skated by each oblivious of the other—two people hurrying on their way to appointments. He was a stride past me when I started my slow tumble to the ice and flattened out, an exercise in futility since by then there was nothing in front of me but a huge expanse of ice. Behind me—though I never saw it since I was sliding out toward the blue line—Gretzky flipped the puck into the open net.

He wanted to do it again. He skated back and, smiling, stood by as I hauled myself up, first on all fours, then one skate under me, and then the big heave that got me upright, teetering briefly; I headed slowly back for the nets.

This time when Gretzky picked a puck out and put it to the blade of his stick and started to move, I went out from the mouth of the cage more warily. I had decided not to fling myself to the ice. "Stand up! Stand up!" my coaches had instructed me firmly. Besides, to get myself up off the ice took too much out of my limited reserves.

Gretzky came straight at me; then just as I thought we might collide he sailed off at a tangent, one of those lateral moves Ted Green had talked about, and I had a brief glimpse of the puck soaring past my hip on its way to the goal.

One more! He wanted the hat trick apparently. But this time as I wearily went out toward him, crouched slightly, he fired the puck twenty feet or so directly into my catcher's glove, right into the folds of it, exactly on target. I could have had my eyes closed. It was as if he had come and handed the puck to me. I raised the glove and looked at the puck gratefully.

"Well, that was very nice of you."

We were skating off the ice together. "One out of three," he murmured with a smile. "Not so bad."

He dropped off to speak to someone motioning from the boards. He leaned over to look at some papers or something to sign. He conducted his businesses on the fly. He certainly had enough to consider. That afternoon I had been told that among the numerous products he sponsored was a wallpaper design—his image was on the wall of countless boys' rooms throughout the Provinces.

As for me, it was more simple; as I stepped up onto the rubber matting that led back down the corridor to the locker room, I thought, "Yes, one for three. Truly not so bad. The old saw. Like the Ancient Mariner, I have stoppeth one of three!"

THAT night the Stanley Cup itself was on display in the anteroom where the Oilers team and the civic dignitaries were waiting to line up and file into the banquet. Two bagpipe players in kilts stood by the bar; their instruments lay collapsed in a corner, the black pipes off at an angle like the horns of killed gazelles. The Stanley Cup was on a low coffee table. Behind it on a sofa sat Wayne Gretzky, staring out between his knees at the cup, tracing the myriad of names on the base with his finger. He was absorbed. The cup itself is an insignificant thing, the size of a football. It was purchased for $48.67 in 1893 and I would suppose of all the trophies—with the possible exception of yachting's America's Cup (which is worth two dollars more than the Stanley and does not even have a bottom) it has had more millions spent relative to its intrinsic value than for any other trophy in sport. It has had its bad moments. In 1905 in Ottawa it was dropkicked into the Rideau Canal; the next day someone went back and fished it out, and now it sits on top of an immense hollow column plated in silver with the names of the winning players over the years engraved on it. There is enough room on the columns, I was told, to absorb the names through the year 1999. I watched Gretzky running his finger among the names. The plan was that he would carry the cup into the banquet, the bagpipes skirling, caught in a spotlight, carrying it aloft over his head much as he had once carried it around the ice surrounded by his teammates when the Oilers beat the Islanders in the 1984 play-offs.

The bagpipe players picked up their instruments from the corner; they puffed them into life and skirls, and in a long column the banquet officials and guests were led into an immense banquet hall, picked out by an arc light as we marched up to a dais. After we were seated, each member of the Oiler team came through the doors accompanied by a young "Junior Achiever," the last of them with Gretzky who was holding the huge cup aloft, so that caught in that intense light it seemed to throw off a luminosity of its own. The crowd, about a thousand of them stretching back into the darkness, rose and roared out their appreciation.

I kept wondering what I was going to say when my turn came to speak. My table companion on the dais told me something about the Junior Achievers program. The idea was to supplant the notion that the only exalted thing to do in the culture was to excel at sports. So these kids had concentrated on starting little businesses; rather than spending their time in gyms, or tennis courts, or hockey rinks, they were entrepreneurs—doing things like decorating Kleenex boxes with bas-relief plastic frogs and selling them. They invented products. They sold stock in their little companies. They went to business leaders for advice. They talked to banks. They learned to keep financial books.

I asked if some of the less successful had to file for bankruptcy—whatever the Canadian equivalent was of Chapter 11.

My table companion laughed and said he doubted it. The young tended to be much more prudent than their elders.

After the coffee had been served, a young man at the dais, about eleven years old, rose and gave a long speech by memory on the value of entrepreneurship at an early age. He quoted a number of people, including Benjamin Franklin. Sometimes he waved his arms abruptly, as if a speaking coach had told him to do so to emphasize a point. After fifteen minutes or so, he sat down to a storm of applause and admiration.

He was followed by a young girl, perhaps a year older, who talked about her company and how she and a few others had started it; she mentioned bottom lines and profit margins. She did not use any notes either. The crowd out in the darkness rose to applaud her.

My turn came. I rose into the blast of a searchlight. The audience was almost invisible in front of me. I mentioned how important I thought the Junior Achievement program was. So many of us dreamed of being professional athletes (the humorist James Thurber had guessed that 95 percent of American males put themselves to sleep at night striking out the batting order of the New York Yankees) and yet it was such a mournful hope. In the United States there were only six thousand athletes—from bowlers to baseball players. Probably more people worked in the thimble-making industry than played professional sports. Besides, those privileged few who played sports were not anxious to let go; openings for newcomers, the rookies, only were available because of a veteran's decrepitude or ineptitude, both indications of failure to which athletes do not admit readily.

The number of people who went into professional sports annually would take up only a portion of the very auditorium in which we were sitting.

I described some of my brief forays into sports as a participatory journalist, and what it was like, and how I envied the athletes their skills and the fellowship, but how I had always left their camps with a faint twinge of relief that I was returning to my own world. Theirs was a curious society which often did not tend to its own. Their careers were short. And once out, they became pariahs, as if what had forced them to drop out might be infectious to those still active. I told them what John Wensink had said . . ." feeling like a gust in the wind."

No, the Junior Achievers had their priorities exactly right. In fact, the hockey players out in the darkness doubtlessly supported the program with a slight twinge of envy since they knew that however glamorous their profession they were stalled in something which would not be of much use later on. On the other hand, the boy who had given the speech quoting Benjamin Franklin was going to be the mayor of Edmonton. The girl could have Saskatoon. I said as much.

But as I spoke, I wondered vaguely if I truly believed what I was saying. Or that anyone else did, for that matter. I could see Gretzky at the table in front of me. The wayward rays from the spotlight glinting off the great trophy illuminated his pale face. I had the sense that hundreds of pairs of eyes were watching him. Sometimes I could see the shadowy silhouette of someone standing up from his table in the shadows of the amphitheater to get a better look. Around the perimeter of Gretzky's table I could see boys crouched with paper and pencils who would leap forward when I was done to cluster around him and then escape back to their tables with the palpable evidence of an autograph that they had been in his presence. His likeness was on the wallpaper of their rooms! How was an eleven-year-old skating on a pond in the winter months to think of putting frogs on a Kleenex box!

I looked into my notes. I cleared my throat.

I did not speak at length of my own hapless experience with Gretzky that morning at the rink. It did not seem appropriate at an occasion which was extolling achievement. The only thing I said about Gretzky was that I knew he achieved great joy from what he did, which was essential to hope for in anything one tried. Gretzky had once said that it was fortunate he lived in a penthouse in Edmonton because if he lived at street level he'd look out and see the kids playing road hockey; he'd go out and join them, and play with such pleasure and intensity that his game on ice that night might suffer. He had said simply about the joys of hockey: "I cannot imagine doing anything else."

I remember how bright it was to stand at the dais in the cone of light from the searchlight, but not so bright I could not see the great Stanley Cup standing in the middle of Gretzky's table. He was not listening. He was still staring at the names on the column as if he could scarcely believe his own was there.

A F T E R W A R D , when the Oilers came to town or out to Nassau, I went to see them—to watch the workings of one of the great mechanisms in sports . . . and Mister Gretzky, of course. Then when the Bruins came down to play in Madison Square I had to see them because my passionate concern for their well-being was still very much there. But things had calmed down considerably. I watched the game in reasonable equanimity. I called up my Zamboni friend.

"Would you like to go to the hockey game tonight?"

"Who's playing?"

"Well, the Bruins are in town. I promise not to be fidgety. I will cheer for them in moderation. I won't pound my feet."

"Well, I just don't . . ."

"I won't leave you sitting there while I visit the locker room after the game. You can come with me. You can peek in the door if you want."

"Well . . ."

"I'll watch the Zambonis with you between periods. I will exult with you about the nice ice. I have found out more about the Zambonis. There are four thousand of them in the country."

"Four thousand!"

"There was a guy in Buffalo who drove home from the rink in one to have lunch until the authorities stepped in. They stopped it because the sight of it caused so much traffic congestion midtown."

"Is that so . . . "

"They have Volkswagon engines in them."

"Oh."

"Guess what. You can order one. You can get one in three months if you order it today. Sometimes in the slack season you can get one within a week! Are you going to come to the game?"

"Well . . ."

"Please."